AN HONEST GUIDE TO WORK

Tips for surviving the modern workplace without losing your mind, or your job*

by RJ FRANK

* results not guaranteed

© 2025 RJ Frank

The moral right of the author has been asserted.

All rights reserved. No part of this publication may be reproduced, stored in a retrieval system, or transmitted in any form or by any means (electronic, mechanical, photocopying, recording or otherwise) without the prior written permission of the copyright holder and publisher of this book, except for brief quotations used in reviews, scholarly works, or as permitted under the Australian Copyright Act 1968.

Published 2025

Cover design by designerbility*

Typeset by Wayne Kehoe

ISBN: 978-0-646-71974-0

Disclaimer: The information in this publication is provided for general informational purposes only. While every effort has been made to ensure its accuracy at the time of publication, the author and publisher assume no responsibility for errors or omissions, or for any outcomes related to the use of this material. This book is not intended to serve as legal or professional advice. Readers should consult appropriate professionals before making decisions based on the content of this book.

*This book is proudly AI free.
A human wrote all of this.
Sorry in advance.*

Dedicated to SH who has had to put up with all my complaining before (and sometimes after) I started putting my thoughts down on paper.

Contents

7	A word from the author
9	Introduction
9	How to use this book
11	Why I am the way I am
19	An introduction to work
23	**Part 1: The system is broken (but there's no escape)**
24	The workplace is a battlefield
26	The average person
33	Givers, takers and fakers (and why you shouldn't listen to me)
42	The 60/20/20 Rule
46	The art of being busy
51	**Part 2: Who you are at work (and why it's weirdly complicated)**
52	Playing the perception game
54	Your job as your identity
57	How to get ahead
63	**Part 3: Navigating coworkers, bosses and bullshit**
64	Luck is the biggest factor in your career
68	Assholes and opinions
72	The CEO is the last person you should ask
76	Your boss probably isn't a leader
82	The best person at the job may not be the best person for the job
86	The Law of Individual Excellence
91	Corporate cliff diving

95	Be friendly but be careful who you befriend
101	Life is a group assignment
107	The art of self-preservation

111 Part 4: Work culture is not what you think

112	The workplace is not a democracy
117	Case study: The Boaty McBoatface paradox
119	Understanding "Priority Number One"
123	Prepare for the propaganda
126	The myth of business efficiency
129	Case study: Inefficiency in practice
132	The meritocracy myth
137	Other helpful terms that might explain what you're seeing
142	If it seems easy, it's because you don't know enough about it
147	Acting like an ADILT
149	Case study: The hole in the wall

153 Part 5: Where do we go from here?

154	The "perfect business"
157	So what's important?
160	You'll be fine (probably)

A word from the author

"Yeah well, y'know, that's just like your opinion man."
–The Dude, *The Big Lebowski*

THE VIEWS SHARED in this book are mine and mine alone. I have tried to capture my own experiences and observations as best as I can but like all experiences, they are subject to my own skewed perceptions and biases.

For my own sake, I have tried to remove any identifying aspects when it comes to individuals, situations and organisations mentioned in this book. I don't do this to try and protect them, but to protect me. My honest belief is that there should be a more transparent way for lowly employees like you and I to get a better understanding of the businesses we might choose to work for and the people we might work with. Sadly, the world and the organisations in it are pretty litigious and punitive.

So that's why I'm protecting myself.

No employer wants to be exposed, and no employee wants to be shamed because of their actions — as much as I would like to do those things — so I have decided to reflect through a slightly misty mirror rather than a fully transparent reflection.

My genuine wish is that one day we will find a more universal way to share the truth about companies and our experiences in them. Whilst "The Organisation" positions itself as powerful, influential and progressive, the truth is that any individual who criticises *one* organisation is likely to find that getting a job in *any* organisation becomes more of a challenge[1].

Frankly, I would also like to be employable in the future in case this book thing doesn't work out, and I'm not going to bite the hand that feeds me, my family, my mortgage broker, my bank manager, my insurance agent, the retail duopoly that I buy my groceries from, my cat's vet, the global conglomerate that owns the local fuel station...

---

1   I will use the term The Organisation to represent any and all organisations. Sometimes it will be specific, sometimes it will be a more generic means through which to reference businesses and workplaces more broadly.

Introduction

How to use this book

I'M FULLY AWARE that authors — like CEOs — can overstate the importance of their role in society, and correspondingly I would hate to overstate the role of *this* author and *this* book. So, to avoid any potential hubris I thought I'd start by giving some practical guidance on how I think this book is best used.

It's worth thinking of it a little like the Bible, the Koran or the Torah.

And by that, I mean you shouldn't treat it as a literal guide through which to live your life. Use it in the same spirit that most of those who choose to tread a religious path use the aforementioned documents — as a broad guide from which to pick and choose observations, anecdotes and lessons that suit your own narrative, your own needs and your own preferences.

Are there bits you don't like? No problem at all! Dismiss those few pages or that chapter or those couple of lines and just move on. Fundamentally disagree with those concepts brought to life through a specific anecdote? Perfect. Just ignore it, put your head down and don't change your behaviour one bit. I even welcome that most popular of pastimes amongst avid readers of religious texts — re-interpreting and moulding the words I have shared in a way that suits your own needs. Just because I quite literally say something it doesn't mean that you can't apply your own lens and reconstruct it in a way that validates your needs, prejudices and biases.

Sometimes I have been as overt as I can be in pulling out the lesson or guidance from the particular area of exploration. Sometimes I've simply laid out my observation of whatever the scenario was or on-shared some advice that has been shared with me. Regardless I have left it to you — the reader — to determine what lesson, if any, you might take out of it. I hand these coming chapters to you and leave them in your care for you to use as you see fit.

This book is not an anti-capitalist manifesto, nor is it an anti-work dog whistle. It is intended to be a collection of observations and stories that represent millions of similar experiences happening at any given moment in any number of working environments. It's a bunch of somewhat conjoined chapters that are intended to open the lid a little of what is happening in offices and boardrooms all over the planet.

So this book will mirror my own CV; somewhat embellished and unlikely to stand up to any kind of detailed scrutiny, and heavily reliant on my self-selected references to bring any level of authority to things. But what it does mean is that I've seen a bit, heard a bit and learnt a bit, and hope to share a bit with you through these pages.

INTRODUCTION

Why I am the way I am

It probably seems incredibly narcissistic to start by talking about myself. But in this instance, I think it's worthwhile sharing with you a little about me, primarily to give you some sense of the lens through which I have experienced the world of work.

Truth be told, I'm not actually a huge fan of work.

I like the "getting paid" bit, but the work stuff itself? I could probably take it or leave it.

I used to take work personally.

Then some years ago I went through a period of complete work-led mental collapse, and it led me to a harsh but necessary realisation.

At the time I was part of a multi-billion-dollar organisation which was one of a small number of businesses that was truly thriving on the back of The Pandemic[2]. The Organisation's sales were growing exponentially and it was being quoted by the government as a true saviour of the economy (first) and community (distant second). The CEO had become a celebrity of sorts for keeping the country entertained and informed through those trying times.

My job (and outrageously ostentatious title) saw me playing a supporting role in all of this. I was one of the members of the team that was sharing updates with customers, working with operational teams to understand and communicate the latest pandemic-induced issue, and providing support to a stressed and stretched group of employees who were on the ground dealing with the ebbs and flows of panic and pandemonium. I felt like I was truly flourishing in a high-speed environment where few

---

2   Much like those people who once referred to The Great War and naively assumed that was the end of things, I'm reluctant to refer to "The Pandemic" because it's likely I'll be made to look a fool in years to come.

of the rules had been written and individual initiative was being encouraged. And I was being respected and acknowledged for it.

Then I was made redundant.

In the middle of a once-in-a-fucking-hundred-year pandemic I was without a job.

I was devastated.

Society and business were in uncharted waters, I had two young kids and a new mortgage. And now, I was out of a job.

The redundancy wasn't based on my performance (obviously), it was definitely part of wider and necessary changes (of course), and we wish you the best of luck in the future (seriously?).

The experience taught me so much about leadership, resilience, ego, humanity, and how businesses and individuals leverage a crisis. It taught me about (unilateral) loyalty, failing (upwards), (extreme) capitalism, and (work) friendships. More on all of that later.

And you know what? It has in some ways helped me be a better employee, a better friend, a better leader and a better person — but maybe not in that frothing sycophantic way that you see smeared across your LinkedIn feed[3]. It made me far more cynical, observant, and critical. It's improved my mental health, and it's improved my approach to work and life.

It also gave me an opportunity to separate myself from my job and look at it more objectively. And I started taking notes. Thus, the idea for this book was born.

This book does not come from a place of hate of work or workplaces or, indeed, capitalism. My honest view is that extreme capitalism, like extreme communism or socialism, is fundamentally flawed. I wouldn't label myself a capitalist or a socialist per

---

3   At time of writing LinkedIn remains one of the few social media platforms that has avoided significant scrutiny. That's not to say it's any good but it has become a proxy for professional networking and open source advice. It also means it is hilariously pro-business and bereft of much of the reality of the working world.

se, but more of a pragmatist. I didn't choose the economic system I live in but like many people, I've done my best to carve out a path that allows me to survive and — potentially — thrive within it. It's not the "16-hour days, motivational quotes, LinkedIn hustle" kind of best. It's more like the "I enjoy financial security, and holidays are fun too" kind of best.

But let's all acknowledge that money truly does make the world go round.

Maslow's Hierarchy of Needs does a pretty good job at outlining what humans need to survive and prosper. And when our entire social and economic system relies on the ability to trade money for stuff — whether physical or service-based — it's pretty clear you need money to meet those needs. Simple as that. And this is what I mean by taking a pragmatic approach to surviving in a capital-driven society.

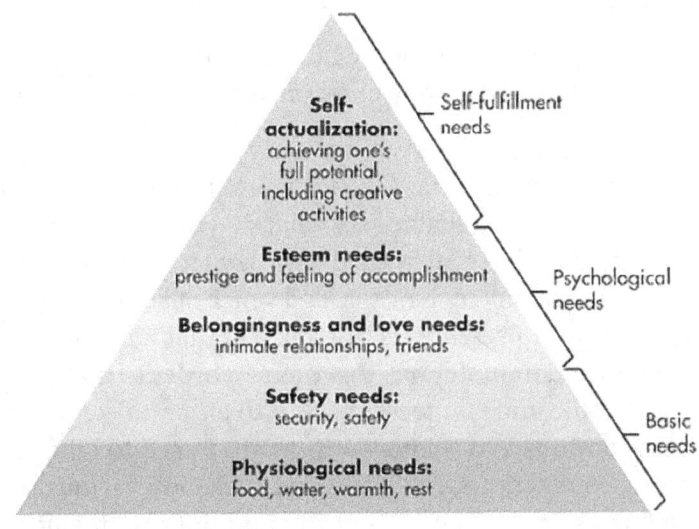

Reference: Maslow, 1943

Interestingly, when you look closely at Maslow's Hierarchy, it becomes clear that many of our basic needs are significantly easier to meet when you have money. Therefore, our ability to reach true self-fulfilment is, in many ways, largely dependent on our access to money. And the most reliable way to get money? Well, it's through work.

It took me a long time to realise a very simple truth: Work is a necessary part of finding comfort in contemporary society. Therefore, I had to find ways to make work benefit me.

Human nature requires us to strive for prosperity. It used to be that prosperity was related to having a full belly and psychological and physical safety. Now our definition of prosperity requires full bank accounts and full garages.

I have fallen victim to the addiction that the hunt for prosperity creates, and for many of us work is the drug of choice. Having said that, I'm not completely immune from the occasional effort to rage against the machine, even if it has been in a kind of guerilla warfare approach versus an all-out conventional war. And this book is part of that asymmetric warfare.

There have also been periods where my addiction has been so strong that it has completely consumed my whole sense of self.

For a fairly significant part of my early career my identity was intrinsically tied up in what I did for work. I used to open conversations with the ever-reliable "so, what do you do for work?" line of questioning in the thinly veiled hope that it would open a door for me to show off my own misguided sense of self-worth created through whatever pretentious title I had at that moment. I'd go to work events and industry get-togethers in order to build my professional profile and connections, and to enter an echo chamber of congratulations and acknowledgement. I used to take pride in how many connections, followers and clicks my various profiles got. Embarrassingly, I even used to hand out my business card on dates to try and impress on the innocent recipient how vital my work was to the successful operation of the economy and the general wellbeing of society at large.

So I have experienced the entire spectrum of how I look at work ranging from "I would give anything not to have to do this" through to "this is my life and I can see nothing beyond it."

It's also clear that my relationship with work wasn't and isn't unique. Whether you're on the frontlines of customer service, the backrooms of hospitality, the inner workings of government or the shopfloor of industry, my story has some parallels with the experiences you will have had or will have somewhere in the future.

Most importantly, my more recent experience reminded me (how did I forget this?) that work is a transaction: your labour for their money. Everything else is superfluous. And that's common across anyone who is part of the working world. Anything you are told differently is "loyalty-washing" and is designed to create an imbalance whereby The Organisation wants to introduce other variables outside of their money in order to get you to work harder. They'll do anything they can to try and extract more output from you, including using terms like "loyalty", "future opportunities" and "aligned values."

You want more out of The Organisation, and The Organisation will do whatever it can to get more out of you.

Somehow we've been convinced that work is the end outcome — or the important bit — of life, and the modern world has us convinced that the world revolves around work. We're told we need to be loyal, we need to be engaged, and we need to be "going the extra mile". Well, that's all designed for capitalism to get more out of you today than yesterday. If you're loyal, engaged or going the extra mile it means that The Organisation is winning in that they're extracting more productivity out of you. They are extracting discretionary effort from you and, by definition, that discretionary effort is over and above what they are paying you for. The party who baulks first is the one that is on the losing side of the "scales of capitalism".

Putting it in simple terms, you want to get the right amount of money (or more, ideally) for the labour you are providing a business. Business, however, wants to get more work out of you than they are legitimately paying you for. They want more revenue for less outgoings, and when push comes to shove, you're a cost in that innocent looking line on a spreadsheet somewhere called "wages". They want to pay the smallest amount possible in wages whilst extracting the largest amount of productivity (and profit) possible.

And your goal? To extract the most out of your employer in the form of payment (wages, share options, bonuses, etc.) to skew the balance in your favour. Those at the top of the tree have done a much better job than you at skewing the scales in their favour. That's what success is. It's not just about the most money. It's actually about extracting the most money possible for the smallest amount of effort.

Want to test this equation? Go right now to your boss or manager or whoever and say to them that you are willing to work *extra* hard next week if they agree to pay you more for that effort. You and I know what the answer will be. It will be some form of "no". It will likely be "we'll recognise your effort with pay increases in the future" or "let's talk about this at salary review time" or "get fucked are you kidding me get back to work for fuck's sake".

What they are saying is that they expect you to work above the requirements of the job for some undefined period *before* they are willing to match that effort with corresponding remuneration. They want you to work harder for them than is warranted by your pay, and they might align your pay with that effort down the track. They are essentially in credit to you, with no obligation to pay up. And that's why most people have to leave their current employer to rebalance the remuneration vs effort scale.

So, back to my own credentials.

Honest truth? I'm a pretty normal wage-slave who's hung around the working world for a couple of decades. Like you I've probably inflated my experience a little too much at times. I've made things up on the fly when talking to customers or my boss or colleagues. I've also spent hours lost in my own mind or on my own device rather than putting the hours in for my employer. I've worked in kitchens and behind bars (the kind you drink at, not the kind where you pay back your debt to society), and I've worked in retail and construction. I've been in big corporations, I've been in start-ups, and I've even been in start-ups in big corporations.

In more recent years the majority of my time has been spent doing all of these things in an office setting as a "middle-manager" (*gasp*), but make no mistake, I've spent countless hours washing dishes and having pans thrown at me by the chef. I've been reprimanded by a cranky middle-aged woman because we didn't have her spoilt 12-year-old's shoe size; and I've run that conversation over again and again in my head around how I should've actually handled that boss or customer or colleague to deliver that genital-tingling sense of supreme justice and righteousness. I've been a victim of inequality, bullying and harassment. I've been promoted, overlooked, landed my dream job and fired.

And I've completely screwed things up, won people over, dropped the ball, delivered on time and seen the best and worst of people and the businesses they work in.

So, it's been a well-rounded and fairly standard experience of the working world.

But what's most important is that I've spent a lot of time watching, interpreting and documenting the actions and words of those around me in a way that's been more objective — at times — than most.

Being made redundant in traumatic fashion and being rehired by that same organisation a week later (unironically), meant that the facade of business had slipped away, and I was now able to *interpret* it rather than simply be *in* it. I was hooked on acceptance and encouragement and hard work and collaboration. I even took pride in having a calendar full of meetings.

And suddenly that was all taken away from me. I found myself blinking upwards into the sunlight with a new sense of self and a realisation I was going to have to do this without the opacity that blind loyalty offered. I started pulling together my notes and my observations in a way that went from being merely for me into some kind of narrative designed to stop the next person from falling into the same cycle of addiction and regret that I have experienced.

Now, I'm a wannabe Sir David Attenborough of the working world. I've seen the best and the worst of the organisational kingdom, and I think I'm kind of OK at documenting those observations in a way that I genuinely hope provides some benefit to you. And if not, it's certainly cathartic to me. Maybe my cadence, richness and resonance don't quite get to the heights of Sir Attenborough, but perhaps an observation or two might start to encroach on his lofty heights of documentary making.

An introduction to work

THE WORKING WORLD is inhospitable. In fact, there's a very strong argument to suggest that having humans involved in "work" at all is a straight up inconvenience.

The vast majority of people who work don't really like it, truth be told, and those who have to pay those working people don't really like doing that either. All in all, no-one is super happy about the concept of work.

There are those people who will try and fool you into believing that the workplace is a modern-day utopia — full of acceptance, shared responsibility, compassion and high fives. You're surrounded by "team members" and "work families" not underlings and minions. Maybe way back in the 1970s they had meetings. Now we have stand-ups, huddles and "actionshops". And managers or bosses? Forget that. It's more like Guild Leads and Endorsers.

Despite what most modern blogs, publications and organisational shamans might tell you, the reality is that the working environment hasn't changed as much as you might think compared to yesteryear. We're still just a semi-random conglomerate of humans trying to create comfort for ourselves and others through gainful employment. Perhaps there's less smoking in the office now, but inevitably the fundamentals of work still remain largely consistent with the version generations before us have had to navigate.

Sure, there are changes brought about by the invention of reverse-cycle air conditioning and digital whiteboards, but most of those changes are cosmetic. Whether you're debating issues on screen, or thrashing things out over your sixth "lite" beer on the back of a napkin in a crowded bar, the reality of the working world is that a lot of it remains the same. We go to work, we complain about our boss or fellow employees, we earn some money, and we go home to our individual lives.

The "good" news is that as a result many things remain consistent and are therefore somewhat predictable. Businesses are still trying to undermine or circumvent child slavery laws, indentured servitude remains rife across the globe, businesses are generally still trashing the environment to maximise production efficiencies and minimise costs, and workplace depression and fatalities are still very much a part of the modern-day working fabric. Workers are still treated as disposable resources, and businesses are actively working against labour laws in order to maximise profits. So yeah, not a lot has changed.

This consistency with the past also means that person-to-person interaction has remained relatively constant and a continued fundamental in how "work" works. Humans naturally like to align themselves with people who share similar outlooks on life, fulfilment and effort. The working environment may evolve through technology and increasingly obscure management techniques, but it still relies on the interaction of people to determine a (sometimes) agreed and unified outcome. Occasionally those same people even universally agree to work towards that outcome. Whether you're building a boat in order to explore (and probably conquer) the neighbouring island or culture or civilisation, or working on that next product to explore (and probably conquer) the next market or vertical or industry, it's still a bunch of people with different perspectives, experiences, expertise and social skills all working (generally) towards an outcome, and guided by some level of authority (although the whipping and shackles are somewhat frowned upon now).

And of course, with the inclusion of humanity in any process comes an inevitable range of complex human-to-human variables and interactions. You can have as many share walls, adaptable working spaces and standing desks as you want, but you can be sure you'll still come across a range of personalities and politics that would look familiar to a jester in an English royal court in 1646[4].

So let me make a commitment to you.

I want this book to be practical. I want you to learn something, and I want you to be better able to comprehend, interpret and survive whatever working environment it is that you find yourself in. Whether it's that monster burger you're serving, that monster acquisition you're leading, or that monster boss you're thinking about strangling, I'll weave in lessons I have learned through my travels or from those around me and provide recommendations and suggestions where it makes sense.

In all my travels through the working world, I've yet to see a training module, management memo or slide deck that provides real insight into the working world, let alone a book. History is written by the winners, and in this case the corporate behemoth is the winner, and we, the workers, are not. There's few, if any, true representations of the working world that aren't coloured by either a large organisation using it to try and drive efficiencies in their "people costs" (aka wages), or by someone trying to squeeze a few hard earned bucks out of you in the hope of handing over some advice that just might give you a slight advantage over your fellow human.

Yeah, there's certainly heaps of books around helping you dress for success in that interview, "how-to" guides about bringing the teachings of great philosophers into your organisation to guarantee effectiveness, tips to create a real estate portfolio using these simple yoga positions, or even the nine secrets of how not to give a f*ck about mindful meditation in order to create irresistible copy for your soap making start-up. But there are very few guides designed to help you to survive and thrive in the wrestling

---

4   For those interested, Charles I was the King of England in 1646. Interesting guy. Lead his country into a civil war, believed his will was the only way, and was largely viewed as tyrannical by the parliament. Probably would've been a fantastic CEO in a more contemporary setting.

match that is the working world. There are very few books that share insights around how things might *actually* work.

Let me be clear: This book does not profess to be entirely comprehensive in explaining how work works. That's too big a task for just one lone voice. Instead, this book is largely a series of anecdotes, observations and insights designed to help you construct your own version of the working world. My hope is it might just offer you a glimpse behind the curtain that other books tend to shy away from.

So why is this important?

Because navigating the working world — whether you're just starting out, trying to make sense of why you left it, or stuck somewhere in between — is often harder than it should be. It's because we all deserve something closer to the truth. Maybe you're looking for insights that don't sound like they were manufactured by a LinkedIn AI bot? Maybe you're tired of being fed one-size-fits-all advice, dressed up as ancient wisdom or startup hustle gospel? Maybe you want to see the messiness of work laid bare, to feel less alone in it, and maybe even to laugh about it?

This book won't fix your job, but it might help you see it and interpret it more clearly. It might remind you that the problem isn't always you — and to give you some tools, stories or sideways perspectives to help you survive it with your health, humour and sense of self intact.

Welcome to a *mostly* honest guide to wherever it is you work, because finding a totally true version is almost impossible.

PART 1
The system is broken (but there's no escape)

The workplace *is* a battlefield

MODERN BUSINESS has tried incredibly hard to distance itself from any comparisons that might exist between it and the concept of war. But try as they might, the signs are very much still there.

There are still plans and headquarters, divisions and objectives. There are leaders and teams, recruitment and training, secondments and missions. It's all there, whether or not it's hidden behind inspirational quotes on the wall or free lunches and gym memberships.

And the reality is that the experience in business can feel like warfare. There are tribes who are in constant conflict with each other, divisions who have taken their positions and won't be moved, and businesses that are in direct competition with each other in order to stake a claim to that territory or market.

So don't be fooled. The language may have changed but the intent has not. You will need to recognise that at times you will be on a battlefield, fighting for your (professional) life. There will be enemies who are looking for any advantage to take you out, and there will be moments where you will share the glory of victory and the pain of defeat with those around you.

You'll feel the cut and thrust of that battle, as tides turn for and against you — individually or as a business. You'll scrutinise enemy decisions to see if it creates a threat or an opportunity for you to conquer or retreat.

You'll see those around you fall, and you'll hold commemorations to recognise their service and sacrifice. You'll see new recruits that need training, so they don't make costly mistakes and charge into the line of fire, and you'll inevitably spend time longing for loved ones back at home.

And, like warfare, there are conventions to how the battle will be fought, and there will be those out there who choose to ignore those conventions to take advantage of any potential opportunity.

There will be periods of relative peace as sides strengthen their defences and work on their next opportunity to attack at a point of weakness. There is research and development into the next innovation that will offer an advantage on the battlefield, there are psyops and battles for hearts and minds on the home front and in enemy territory. And truth is often the first victim once conflict starts to arise. Sometimes there will be mutinies, and other times there will be a complete clean-up across the ranks. And like war, when the tide has turned or the pressure is overwhelming, you too may become cannon fodder.

The average person

THE CONCEPT OF THE 'average person' is kind of scary when you think about it.

Now the statisticians and sociologists can wine you and dine you with snappy infographics and TEDx talks about the actual "average person", but I've created this image in my head of that person that has pretty much served my purposes for several decades. Don't get me wrong, it's not a personification designed to give me an inflated sense of worth or intellectual superiority — actually, it's the opposite. I use it to anchor myself back into the centre of the society I am part of. We naturally live in echo chambers of our own design. We choose our friends, our opinions, and our sources of information, and inevitably we end up self-referencing based on our own perspective and experiences. We think our experience is normal and the norm. Well, it's likely complete bullshit. And that's where my "average person" concept comes in.

My version of the average person is someone saddled with debt, thinking about their next holiday, worried about their family, and working in a job that is sometimes engaging but is mainly a means to an end[5]. And that end includes a house or apartment — rented or otherwise — that they're not quite happy with. They're inevitably looking for the next product, the next upgrade, the next social opportunity or the next chance to just get away. They generally dislike people telling them what to do, are generally cynical

---

[5] I am very conscious that this definition of "the average person" is so incredibly skewed to a — most likely — Western society where we have the privileges and material benefits that come with that. The reality is that it's reflective of the society within which I have grown up and spent my working life, and therefore my reference point for how I think about the average person. I think it would be an incredibly interesting exercise to review and rewrite this whole book in the context of a variety of social constructs. For now, forgive me as I write — quite selfishly — from the context of my own experience of "the average person".

about brands and government and big business and are eking out whatever enjoyment they can get from life.

It's quite a contrast to what the HR and Marketing teams will have you believe.

Now don't get offended, I'm not describing you. I'm describing the average person for the purposes of reminding myself of what some people find important. In fact, it's partly self-reflective. If it does sound a bit like you, then great, it validates my assumptions, but it also grounds me back in the complex world that each person I cross paths with inhabits.

Now take this concept of average and expand it. Can you imagine if I listed every facet and dimension of this hypothetical "average person"? Like their political persuasions, their mental health status, their views on coriander and abortion and private education? What about if I started adding in their cultural context or their sexual preferences? Their learned experiences from childhood? Their physiological response to conflict? Or even their favourite colour (surprisingly important in the world of marketing by the way)?

Hopefully I've started to illustrate for you how complex the concept of "normal" really is. There's no standard here despite everyone's best efforts. There's no single unifying element across the community. I mean just look at politics. Even the most loved political parties in the Western world might — at best — win 55% of the popular vote (excluding those oligarchies and authoritarian governments that feature the 99.8% approval ratings). That means that just about every second person thought that the outright winner was shit or disagreeable in some way...at best.

This mental model helps remind you of the complexity of the perspective and understanding of each person you find yourself in a room with. People aren't like you, they aren't like me, and they aren't like each other. While the work environment may (or may not) dull some of the extremes of humanity, it won't bring everyone into line. Remember, you might be the outlier in some aspect or another when you bring together a group of people. And one thing that's treated me well, especially in a new environment where you're trying to get a gauge of those around you, is to assume — initially anyway — that you may be the dumbest person in the room.

Why is any of this important?

You are inevitably going to meet a huge cross section of humanity in the working world. Some good, some bad, and some downright (emotionally and mentally) ugly.

You'll meet the overeager, the rageful, the outright lazy and the consistently delightful. You'll see those who are malicious, those who would give the shirt off their own back to help, and those who wouldn't piss on you if you were on fire (just ask anyone who has worked in retail or hospitality). There will inevitably be some people and personality types that you'll come to enjoy watching as they go about their work — for better or for worse — and others who will challenge your fortitude. For instance, I particularly enjoy the contribution of the "all-knowing, any-subject-of-their-choice expert" and the "enthusiasm-draining long-term seat warmer". You'll undoubtedly come across versions of these people in your own travels through the paid labour world, and there aren't enough pages in this book to cover the breadth of personalities you'll cross paths with during your working life[6].

But the critical thing is that the working world is a tapestry of different people with different personalities, perspectives and biases. Those perspectives and biases will be both obvious and discrete, and as varied as the DNA of each individual you come across. Any given digital or physical room you're in during your working life will have a huge spectrum covering age and gender and cultural context and — frankly — intelligence.

It's actually that final dynamic that I want to focus on.

---

6   See my chapter on psychometric testing, pigeon-holing and identity assumptions later on if you want to understand my perspective on these personality tests and their intentional efforts to typecast you and everyone around you.

The concept of intelligence in the work environment is an interesting one. Intelligence comes in many forms. There are also a number of differences between being smart and being intelligent. I don't have time to review the official definition of smart (I've got a book to write) but in my mind being smart is about "brute knowledge". It's a case of knowing lots of things about a range of topics. The relevance of that knowledge, the ability for the individual to adapt the relevance and application of that knowledge to a certain scenario, and the ability to share that knowledge in a way that is engaging, is what I consider "intelligence". It's often referred to as emotional intelligence. Intelligence — as far as I'm concerned — is about understanding the context of your own knowledge, the environment you're in, and the best way to share that knowledge in a respectful and relevant way that contributes to the outcome you're all working towards.

The world is full of lounge chair critics and experts. There are those who are full of advice about what that specific professional sportsperson or coach should've done, those who are willing to air their confidently incorrect views about science or art or society on social media, and those colleagues who are willing to share their perspective on any specific subject despite their seemingly minimal actual learnt or understood experience. Humanity has been provided a range of platforms through which to share our views, and now that assumption has started to leak into the working world.

Every meeting, every informal discussion, every briefing, every class and every work event becomes another opportunity for someone to share their irrelevant opinion or experience or to just ask something really fucking dumb. Now the more sensible amongst us will know that lunch or the end of the shift, or just plain efficiency and the need to get on with it, will mean we keep our trap shut or — at worst — ask that question that will clarify the task at hand in order to get it done faster or more efficiently. But there are plenty out there who are blissfully wandering through life right now and see that moment of silence as their opportunity to reveal their ineptitude and lack of awareness. And sometimes, they won't even wait for a moment of silence. They'll kick the meeting off by revealing their stupidity, as you're having a coffee during a break, or when the floor is opened up to questions.

So, assume you're the dumb person, until such time as others reveal themselves to be even less capable, less proactive or more easily confused. Let them make the faux pas, the stupid observation or the "no shit Sherlock" comment.

But do it within reason.

Don't lose your voice or fail to understand the task at hand because you were too shy, or simply let others take the glory when you should've spoken up. This isn't permission to clam up or shut down. In fact, it's permission for you to think before you open your mouth, consider the needs and context of those around you, and, most importantly, to observe others to make sure you're adding to the conversation, not taking away from it. With confidence must come competence, so give yourself the chance to understand where you fit in the pecking order when it comes to intuition, logic and relevance.

You should also keep in mind that work is not life, and life is not work. You are seeing just a tiny part of someone's complex and vast humanity.

Despite the best efforts of the business world, people are reluctant to bring their "whole self" to a working environment[7]. You're only seeing a glimpse, a preview, or a single dimension of their total personality. It's such a minute part of their existence that you should be careful not to extrapolate things out too broadly. It's so simple to use one interaction to draw judgement on an individual. That's fine when you're in the line at a fast food restaurant or

---

7   The most humiliated and reviled I have ever felt in the professional environment was when I brought my "true self" into the workplace. It seems my willingness to criticise, my lack of sycophantic tendencies towards management and a complete disdain for authority are not conducive to ongoing success in the working world. I have now learnt to develop and refine a "work version" of myself to better align with the demands of my professional progression.

sitting next to them on public transport, but in the working environment your relationship is more than just transactional. These people around you can and will influence your fate.

So, while you may be quick to judge, remember that they too are judging you, and you would likely want them to consider far more about you beyond an individual interaction before drawing conclusions about who you are as a person.

It's also worth remembering that reality and the law of averages will guarantee that you will cross paths with people who are malicious, mean, dim-witted and conniving, as well as those who are jubilant, energising, intelligent and savvy, so be prepared for all of those potential interactions and intersections.

The world is not logical or predictable, and neither are the people you will inevitably cross paths with.

But the one variable that unites this broad spectrum of humanity is that you are crossing paths with them in a working environment. You're united in the fact you're working for someone or something (AI overlords anyone?) and sharing some kind of blood oath that you'll put in work for some degree of financial remuneration[8]. You probably didn't choose to do it alongside them, and they likely didn't choose to do it alongside you. But here you are.

Now, whilst the modern workplace isn't quite as dramatic as an ancient Roman gladiatorial battlefield, you are — like it or not — in some kind of competition with those around you[9]. You're being judged and compared in terms of your workload, your output, your ability to solve problems, your effectiveness in getting the job done, or perhaps just on how amicable you are to deal with (this is often, and unironically, the most important attribute that people will look for).

And the fastest way to slide down the inevitable totem pole of

---

8   Author's note: Unpaid internships — like indentured servitude — should be illegal.

9   There are definitely war-like elements to the working world. See "The workplace is a battlefield" for more revelations on that front.

employee rankings is to know too much. By giving the impression that you're a know-it-all, or that you're too hasty, or that you can't listen and learn, you'll very rapidly give those who are judging you a clear indication that you're rash and arrogant.

Finally — and this advice has stood me in good stead — looking like an idiot is a powerful incentive to just bite your tongue until you know enough not to look like a fool.

PART 1: THE SYSTEM IS BROKEN (BUT THERE'S NO ESCAPE)

Givers, takers and fakers (and why you shouldn't listen to me)

THERE IS A NEVER-ENDING spectrum of different personalities you'll come across during your time as a working Joe or Jane, and each will bring their own context to any given situation or interaction. If you're looking for an empirical data point to help you appreciate the vast breadth of humanity, then I'd go with around 8 billion — or roughly the population of the entire world — given that each and every individual you deal with will have some level of uniqueness in their personality and approach to work. Maybe we could rule out kids so that number drops dramatically to around 5 billion variations.

But the vastness of humanity is in conflict with our need to be able to categorise people in a way that allows us to prepare for our dealings with them in the working world. That diversity of perspective, experience, cultural context and biases makes it dangerous to generalise whole groups of people, but as humans we like organisation, simplicity and familiarity. There is sometimes a requirement to try and put people into buckets in order to adapt how you might work with them and create the best outcome, or to avoid catastrophe.

With that in mind I've come up with a basic model — black and white to a fault — that I use to try and categorise the personas and drivers of the people that I have worked with. It's far from perfect, and it does intentionally simplify things with the sole intent of trying to help you understand how best to work together or interact with another person or group of people. I hope you use these very basic categorisations with the spirit that they're intended — as a simple rule of thumb to try and interpret those around you.

These definitions are a distillation of personas into their most single-minded form. They're not designed to be comprehensive or succinct — as I've said humanity is too broad a spectrum for that. You may even recognise yourself in some of these personality types, and it's human nature to adapt to the circumstances around you. I know I have fallen into any of these criteria at different times, or with different people, throughout my career. Use the following as a helpful framework through which to try and interpret the needs and perspectives of the people you'll encounter.

Givers

Givers are often the true engine room of any business. They give of their time and expertise and have a natural intuition and drive that means they generate fulfilment through the delivery of work and seeing the success of those around them.

When Givers are at their best, they like to see growth in their colleagues and business, and they create internal satisfaction by helping lift those around them. They create camaraderie and collaboration to get work done. They have a strong internal drive that can manifest itself as wild enthusiasm or myopic focus.

Givers are not all perfect though, and there are some potential pitfalls of this kind of personality and approach to work.

Givers can end up in a "battery hen"-type situation where they are seen as a resource from which to simply extract work and output. This can lead to them being overloaded ("Get Giver to do it, they're always reliable and love taking on new responsibilities"), under recognised and ultimately disenfranchised by a business that destroys their will to contribute.

For that reason, they often end up working in consultancy firms as juniors and analysts.

Givers can let their good nature get in the way of managing their workload, and their conscientiousness will see them spiral into a greater and greater sense of anxiety as they struggle to take on an ever-increasing burden. A directionless Giver is also a challenge. They can create work in a vain attempt to self-sustain their need for completion and recognition. This can lead to work that duplicates effort, doesn't achieve an outcome or is simply distracting for those around them.

As with all things, there is a spectrum of Givers. The perfect Giver is near self-sufficient and only requires very occasional supervision. They're keen to share their knowledge, bring others in to help support them in building their own skill set, and are reliable.

When a Giver "goes wild" they're disruptive to others and can be bull-headed and single-minded about how they achieve their goal — at the detriment of relationships and other work that needs to be done. They can become busybodies who are so focused on the job at hand that they can over complicate the task, and they require constant oversight to keep them working within their lane.

The remedy to being a natural Giver is to ensure you have a voice. As the workload increases to a point of being unwieldy, it's necessary to clearly articulate the impacts of that overwork or unrealistic burden. It's also important not to inadvertently take on work from others, lest you lose your own internal drive. It's also critical to ensure that you don't become myopic in the tasks you are trying to achieve, and that you remain mindful of the needs and priorities of those around you.

Or you could go and work in a consultancy and ignore all of this sage advice.

Takers

Takers often make great managers. Not great as in "good for the company" but more of a "know how to work their way into a management role" kind of way. They are focused on output only for the benefit of leveraging it to validate their existence or to build another rung in the ladder in their climb to the top. They often have low awareness because their outlook is so driven by recognition and reward. Those around them are a means to an end and the output of a Taker can be incredibly limited. They thrive on the work that Givers provide and have a semi-symbiotic relationship with them in order to leverage their hard work to drive recognition and output for themselves.

Behind every good Taker is an army of used and abused Givers who have had their work, enthusiasm and good will sucked from them to progress someone else's opportunities.

The upside to Takers is they can be great at coordinating, albeit with limited tangible contribution and questionable intentions. They can bring people together to deliver work, primarily because it makes them look good or gives them further leverage with which to promote themselves. They'll often dress this up as a sense of conscientiousness. They might even make you feel good about it — but make no mistake, it's internal drive that motivates them and their modus operandi is to take from you so they can give to their boss. Strong self-promotional skills and intense relationship development with those in power create the Power Taker. You'll work for one in the future...

And of course, the downside to Takers is clear. You are a means to an end; one more tool they can use to help leverage themselves into the next promotion or the next "well done" from more senior management. They often have an inexplicable level of influence in businesses, brought about by their willingness to critique everything around them, whilst still shaping those more diligent and conscientious than them into delivering an outcome that they position as their own. They eat their young, rule the roost and generally see everyone around them as non-playable characters in this game they call work.

When dealing with Takers it is critical to ensure that you can provide visibility of the work you are doing beyond the Taker themselves. It may be through sideways engagement, or by driving awareness of the role you have played in the creation of that slide deck, idea or solution to an influential audience. If you find yourself caught in the all-absorbing vortex of a Taker, you may need to reach out to other influential teammates and managers to ensure that you're recognised for your effort.

Unless of course you're a Taker yourself, in which case you'll be pretty adept at making sure people know what you've been up to.

Fakers

Incapable of independent thought, Fakers are largely in over their head in terms of expertise or leadership capability, and generally wildly inappropriate for the role they have[10]. Fakers have somehow found their way into their role through excellent execution of their influencing skills more typical of a Taker but have also combined that with a dose of nepotism, preferential treatment, longevity or a simple fear of what might happen if they're not promoted. They might have leveraged these Machiavellian skills to secure a corner office, regular appearances on the speaking circuit, and to convince IT to install a sports management sim or two on their company issued laptop.

The hallmarks of a misdirected Faker are also relatively easy to spot when you know what you are looking for: somewhat confusing directives to teams, inane and frustrating emails that lack relevance to the issues at hand or directives that instantly complicate the work already underway.

The "high intensity" Faker can often be viewed as a little old school, stick up for issues that have long been resolved and put to bed, have a hugely inflated sense of self-importance, and think they're way savvier than those around them. They can often project themselves into a role as the "elder statesperson" or the "deeply knowledgeable and experienced expert" and are dismissive of anything that might be seen as progressive or contemporary. Of course, the world has likely moved beyond their reach but that doesn't stop them from sharing their unwanted opinion on matters where their expertise is questionable.

On the lower end of the scale, a Faker may well have plenty of self-awareness and be smart enough to just keep cashing that cheque. Their days are made up of "meetings" with no firm stat-

---

10   See "The Peter Principle" in the next chapter.

ed agenda (generally outside of the office and for many hours at a time), staring aimlessly at their computer, chatting to colleagues about the weather or that sport team or the current affair of the day, and then quietly picking up their bag and heading off when it's not too early and not too late. They're in a holding pattern and they know it — looking for that golden handshake or impending retirement. Your success, and the success of those around you is superfluous to their own needs.

Generally, I've found that most businesses have a way of "promoting" Fakers out of real positions of authority. They may end up with titles like "Strategic Projects Lead" or "Innovation Director." Or they work in HR.

Whilst Givers are largely an asset to a business, and Takers are likely to rip the soul out of teams and team members in their endless pursuit of self-serving serotonin, Fakers sit right in the middle. Their ability to cause damage is largely limited by their willingness to risk their relatively comfortable position.

Fakers need to be appeased, but not followed. They need recognition, but not complete compliance. And most importantly they probably just need to keep to themselves so as not to destroy the natural order of things and to make a mess of your calendar and inbox.

And why none of this matters

I'm deeply aware that this framework of Givers, Takers and Fakers is in complete contradiction to my opening remarks in this chapter. I've rambled on about the dangers of putting the vast breadth of humanity into some deeply flawed framework to simplify your working life, only to share with you how you can quickly define people on some overly simplified behavioural criteria. It remains the case that humans are too complex to categorise in such a simple fashion, and I'm going to tell you why.

You should take all of this guidance — and any other attempts to suggest people can be easily defined by a few basic characteristics — with a wheelbarrow of salt.

Organisational psychologists, human resource specialists, management consultants and various other potentially toxic opinion holders (including authors with a severe case of imposter syndrome), have all made a career and — more importantly — a revenue stream out of trying really damn hard to put everyone into tidy little boxes. These boxes come in a variety of formats, shapes and names. Some will define you as an owl or an eagle, others will have you on a bell curve or defined by how spiky your circle graph is. You'll be a Dominator or Reformer, a Controller or Supporter, or maybe you'll even be a Giver or a Faker (gulp).

But let's put all that psychometric profiling aside for a second.

Imagine, if you will, that you had to come up with eight buckets into which you must be able to drop all of humanity. Next you have to develop criteria that allows you to sort the entire human race into those same buckets. You can choose any dimension of their physical, social, cultural or mental identity that you want.

So good luck. You've only got 8 billion more people to go (at time of publishing).

Now I get it, there are so many dimensions to a single human it would be IMPOSSIBLE to drop them into just a single defining bucket. So, I'll make it easier for you again. You don't have to define that human by anything other than their aesthetics. No need to worry about their socio-economic circumstance or their psychological nuances. All you have to do is to come up with eight different categories into which you can drop all of humanity based purely on their physical composition.

Firstly, this whole exercise has a little bit of a eugenics feel about it. If you think this task is possible, you may actually be a little racist. Or you may in fact be someone who is well placed to come up with an identity model through which to helpfully categorise EVERY FUCKING PERSON IN THE WORLD INTO BUCKETS.

It just doesn't work. There's no unifying element that runs through the entire population that allows you to drop them into discrete buckets. And there's an even lower likelihood that you could then make assumptions about how they will behave or interact with each other in the future based on these eight defining features.

And so it is with personality tests and psychometric analysis of the workforce.

For me, this feels like the equivalent of defining all food as either sweet or savoury. There's so much nuance. I'm pretty sure the whole concept of Thai cuisine — as a single example — is to challenge our assumptions about sweet and savoury. How many of the nuances of flavour and ethnicity would you miss if you just had a couple of options in which to categorise food? Likewise for trying to put humanity — infinitely more complex than food — into a few clearly defined categories.

To do so severely limits your ability to effectively understand and engage with a huge diaspora of people. I've been pigeon-holed in my career on several occasions as being anti-authoritarian, righteous to a fault, disagreeable and cynical, and it's disengaging and deflating[11]. It seems to me that personality and psychometric tests are by definition designed to pigeon-hole people into mental and behavioural frameworks to define cause and effect. If Suzie is an "Owl" (whatever the fuck that means) then the helpful one-pager you've been handed says she's going to be logical, questioning and precise, but that she's also going to struggle to move forward if she doesn't have all the data. OK, so you're telling me you are able to summarise Suzie's entire approach to life and work because she answered 20 multiple-choice questions on your shitty website and now has to deal with those vast assumptions for the rest of her working career? It's nothing more than a modern-day version of phrenology and should and will be dismissed as such in future decades[12].

---

11   These are all clear misinterpretations of me and my philosophical approach to work, as supported by my commentary in this book.
12   Phrenology (sometimes called Eugenics in mid-World War 2 Germany) is a

So be careful when taking these tests and assuming too much out of their results. Like my framework on the nature of those I've worked with, they're bound to be full of errors, inaccuracies and dangerous assumptions.

---

pseudoscience that looks at measuring the bumps and lumps and broader dimensions of the skull to determine mental faculties and character traits of the individual. In my humble opinion methods like astrological signs, aura analysis and numerology are much more effective means of determining a person's professional and behavioural nuances.

The 60/20/20 Rule

THERE ARE A RANGE of capabilities and skill sets on display in any organisation and within any individual. There are those who excel at their job, and like in any normal distribution curve, there are those who are a walking calamity. That's why the 60/20/20 Rule can be helpful, noting that there is no scientific research behind this other than my very deep observation of the people I've worked with across a number of industries. From bar staff to doctors and engineers (of various persuasions and practicalities), this rule of thumb has stood up to many years of my own scrutiny and review.

Chances are that you will probably recognise these archetypes in whatever business you ply your trade, and perhaps even in your own performance. The intention is not to criticise individuals (who knows what may be affecting their performance on any given day) but instead to better help you notice the patterns and dynamics at play in your workplace, and to caution you so that you can avoid getting crushed by someone else's incompetence.

The Middling Sixty

About sixty per cent of the people you'll come across are absolutely capable. They're pretty consistent deliverers, largely reliable and are able to contribute to the task at hand with the right level of support and guidance. They make up the large majority of people you'll come across.

Their ability to do the job does not necessarily correlate with them being good people, but from an organisational perspective they're all good insofar as getting the job done.

You'll work with them, laugh with them, come to rely on them, and may even go so far as having lunch with them.

The Inspiring Twenty

These people are just excellent at what they do. They've got intuition, expertise and knowledge when it comes to doing the job. Businesses often hang their reputation, their profitability and their longevity off this twenty percent. They're a lightning rod for good work, they're self-sufficient and are often the catalyst for positive business momentum.

They are also critical mentors and are often natural leaders. They have an approachable style, a willingness to share their knowledge, and they are (generally) held in high regard by managers, peers and teams. Find these people, stick with them, build your rapport and reap the benefits that come with working alongside someone as capable as them.

Sometimes they might even take you with them as they progress their career.

The Intolerable Twenty

Bringing up the tail are that twenty per cent of an organisation that are downright dangerous and a complete blight on any business. They're clumsy or naive or dangerously ego-driven. Maybe even all of the above. They cross the line, avoid accountability and shift blame. They can be arrogant to the point of complete myopia. They're a hazard to the people around them (physically and mentally) and can destroy any internal or external goodwill. Strangely, there is no correlation between danger to an organisation and seniority, so you're likely to find this cohort unhelpfully sprinkled throughout a business from top to bottom.

When dealing with this group of intolerable peers it's important to protect yourself. Whether that's protecting your time, your energy or your reputation, it's vital to avoid being dragged into their gravitational pull.

And where might I find these people?

So now that I have shared my highly scientific definition of all the people who have ever participated in paid (and sometimes unpaid) employment, it's worth taking a moment to look at the application of the 60/20/20 Rule through the lens of seniority.

There is a common trope, wheeled out by business media and by generations best identified by their ability to purchase residential property, that suggests there is a clear logic to how people get ahead in business. Namely, they'd suggest that smart people go up, and not-so-smart people sink to the bottom. To be more specific, they propose that the Inspiring Twenty would naturally find themselves at the top, the Middling Sixty would sit firmly in the middle of any organisation, and the Intolerable Twenty would find themselves entrenched at the bottom (or even on the outside) of any functional workplace.

Well, my experience suggests that this is one of the biggest fallacies known to humankind.

There is quite literally zero correlation between how good people are at their job and how senior they are in business. The idea of a meritocracy at work is a myth[13]. Some of the most hostile, unintelligent and illogical people I have ever met have been major decision makers in business. Some have even run the entire operation.

And some of the kindest, most adept and intelligent people have been the ones left to interpret and action those very same illogical decisions somewhere in the bowels of the business. In fact, you might go so far as to suggest that there is a higher likelihood of coming up against the Intolerable Twenty the further you get up the structure of an organisation, given skills like avoiding blame or accountability, being myopic in their focus, and being driven by ego rather than any other humanistic trait are often admired in many "leadership" circles. But it would be a braver person than me to say that outright.

---

13   See the chapter on The Meritocracy Myth later in this book.

So, my advice to you is this: never assume someone more senior than you is better at their job (or potentially even your job) until you have verifiable, third party endorsed validation of that fact. And be comfortable with the fact that there is no escaping the vast range of humanity wherever you may be in your employment journey.

The art of being busy

BUSYNESS IS LIKE a currency in the work environment. You can exchange it for a range of occupational benefits if you're strategic about how you use it. You can use it to pay to get into or out of meetings. It's a key bargaining chip in promotion or remuneration conversations. It's probably the most important chip you can throw on the table when it comes to getting more people to help you, more money to pay for things, and more authority to make decisions.

It's also social equity in the workplace. You can get out your big swinging "busyness" appendage and have a measuring contest with everyone else. They'll gawk at it, admire it and talk about it in quiet corners of the office. "Oh my God, did you see how overwhelming it was? It was huge. There's no-one who could handle that as well as them. How they can walk around with that thing is just a miracle!" they'll say. They'll talk about it at home, at their friends' barbecue, and — especially — when they're lining up for coffee. "They are just so busy! What an absolute miracle worker. I want to be just as busy as them one day. And did you see their calendar when they discretely screen-shared it in that meeting!"

Being busy is a bit like having a big, fancy, impractical four-wheel drive. Everyone will act impressed to your face when you first bring it out, but when you leave and they've had the opportunity to objectively assess it, they're definitely going to be talking about how ridiculous and unnecessary it is - how over the top it seems, given your obvious lack of actual need for it, and how there's no way they would want to be in your position. They'll probably also acknowledge that you're a bit of an attention hog, and that you've convinced yourself it's necessary and a not-insignificant part of your identity.

The thing is that "being busy" is completely manufactured. It's a mental construct rather than a practical measure of how much stuff you have going on. In fact, it's probably indicative of a fault in someone rather than anything to aspire to.

It may be that you have mistaken movement for action.

I've seen great leaders balance full calendars, a variety of team members, a corporate acquisition, a dog and a fast-growing lawn with aplomb. I've also seen leaders who can't say no, commit to it all and fill their calendar with endless meetings with no clear outcome and an inevitable list of follow ups and circle backs and regroups. Only one variation of these leaders has driven real results, tangible outcomes and business benefits. And it's not the one who's providing ambiguous feedback on the same set of slides they've seen for the fourth time with an urgent meeting they have to head to so sorry we didn't come to a conclusion but let's hope that the next meeting we have in two weeks is the one where we really nail it.

I have a counter view in terms of "busyness". Whereas some see it as a badge of honour, for me it's an insight into a mindset that struggles to balance and — sometimes — remove competing priorities and work. It's an insight into a manager or an individual who doesn't have the fortitude or relationship skills to say no, or to ask for more help, or to say to managers and leaders that enough is enough, and that the sheer volume of work that they're proposing is unachievable or overwhelming. For me, being busy is a peek behind the curtain of someone who works inefficiently, who is indecisive, and who lacks the means through which to keep in check the expectations that sit on their shoulders. "Busyness" is an outcome of an organisation that can't define and distribute work effectively, and of an individual who lacks the capacity — consciously or unconsciously — to manage the people and tasks around them.

It may also be a sign of someone who creates a sense of fulfilment or importance by creating work around them, and for those under them.

So when you hear someone who constantly complains about

workload, or who carries their sense of being busy like a Sheriff's badge, then you should resist the urge to heap on them the respect, gratitude and martyrdom they are inevitably looking for. Instead see them as what they are — someone who is too inefficient, to ineffective or too cowardly to resolve their workload, or too non-committal to move work forward or make decisions.

Be advised though, busyness does still hold incredible cache in the workplace. Now I'm not going to admit to managers or peers that I am cruising and working well within my capacity. Instead, I'm going to slowly undo my fly and expose my busyness for all to see if they ask me to. This is the art of presenting yourself as busy, whilst not being busy. "Schrodinger's Busyness" if you will.

Like real currency in an economic system, the currency of "busyness" in an organisational setting is fundamental to your ability to achieve some form of success. As a result, it can't be ignored. For some of us the idea of being seen to be busy will be instrumental in our ability to progress in business. Rarely will someone be promoted if they are seen to be cruising along and never getting out of second gear. In fact, it's likely to have the inverse effect on your ability to ask for or receive that next promotion. So we must portray some level of busyness in order to progress. This is the "why" of being busy. Find that balance of being perceived to be busy whilst having a manageable workload and you will put yourself in the sweet spot when it comes to your opportunities for future advancement. Many of your peers and managers will have already found this sweet spot, and so it's important for you to be able to do this too.

The additional benefit of maintaining a facade around your own busyness is that it will impact on the likelihood of you being given additional tasks and responsibilities by those around you. If you're seen to be delivering whilst admonishing the world and those around you for demanding so much of your time and effort, you rapidly decrease the likelihood of being tasked with more to do.

Use busyness as your own leverage. Ironically, it can be used to free up your time. From declining meetings due to clashes, through to handballing that highly demanding additional task that seems to be floundering on the project sidelines, busyness is a tool that can play a significant role in freeing up your own capacity. As you progress it can even be used to ask for additional people and time. This is the game that people around you are already playing, so why not play the game yourself?

PART 2
Who you are at work (and why it's weirdly complicated)

Playing the perception game

THERE COMES A POINT in every job when you realise you're being watched — not in a creepy surveillance way (well, maybe), but in the way people quietly assess who you are and what kind of person you're trying to be. And chances are, you're trying to figure that out too.

We angst so much about the perception we create in the work environment, and that is particularly pronounced when some aspect about your working environment has changed.

For instance, let's imagine you suddenly become the manager or leader of a team. It may be that you suddenly reassess your haircut, or clothes, or manner in which you speak to those who were once your peers. You may suddenly turn up a little earlier, leave a little later, and swear a little less. You might even begin to mix with slightly different people in the workplace and handle those conversations about your job in a different way when you're gathered around the barbecue, watercooler or birthday cake.

And if you're one of those people who is saying to themselves "success/authority/power/money won't change me" then good on you but you are in the vast minority (or deluded).

Impressions have a huge impact and gravity in the workplace. I've worked alongside people who have been promoted simply *because of* how they appear while amazing people are overlooked for promotions for the same reason.

Remember this: to better adapt to the expectations of your role, you are changing elements of your personality, approach and appearance to try and influence the perceptions of those around you. It's as simple as that. And there's a flipside to this: people will assume things about you regardless of your intent.

Humans are absolutely infested with conscious and unconscious biases. The way you push your glasses back up on your nose? Douche-bag move. The way you say hi in virtual meetings? Painful and embarrassing.

And this is just the beginning. These are cosmetic behavioural observations. Add to this deep-seated biases on body shape, religion, ethnicity or who-the-fuck-knows-what-and-why and you are walking into an absolute firefight of objective and subjective perceptions and perspectives about you.

It's terrifying, but it's reality. Some choose to ignore it and remain proudly independent; others will adapt and change or let it consume them and spend a large part of their physical and mental reserves trying to grapple with it.

There is no simple answer to this conundrum of having to appease the biases of those you will cross paths with in the working world. The reality is that people will carry legitimate and illegitimate perceptions about you, all created with or without your direct input.

So, my response to the inevitable question around how you should manage the juxtaposition between fitting in whilst inevitably being judged on aspects that you can't understand or change is this: what are your values? What's important to you and non-negotiable in terms of how you represent yourself at work? For some people, the answer will be: "I'm willing to change anything and sacrifice everything", while for others it will be: "I'm a strong and independent person and I won't change for anybody." Both answers are legitimate — just be aware of which response will get you further in your place of work.

Your job as your identity

EARLY IN MY CAREER I often conflated my identity with my job. It's so incredibly pathetic now I think of it.

When I met new people, I would gradually steer the conversation towards jobs and work just so I could quickly tell people what it was I did for a living, as though it was some noble cause that should evoke awe and respect.

You see, I had fallen victim to the social prompts that I had seen on television screens and across generations before me, where people would interpret their nobility and social authority based on the job that they had. I had a bastardised illusion of important looking people in formal attire gathering around a fireplace with glasses of sherry, chortling whilst helping themselves to hors d'oeuvres and narrow necked champaign glasses, all explaining the importance of the work they did as doctors and lawyers, politicians and professors[14]. I had somehow — perhaps subconsciously — associated social status and respect with my own vocation.

I would leap at every question, indulge myself in humorous anecdotes about my colleagues and peers and projects, courteously present my counter points to other equally knowledgeable businesspeople, and provide some wide-ranging insight into industry and economics that would end in rounds of applause and slaps on the back. I was the total worth of my job, and my job was the total worth of me.

The reality, of course, is very different, and once I had removed my rose-tinted glasses it became clear that droning on about my job was one of the most tedious and alienating aspects of my personality.

---

14   Strangely this internal image never included the idea of being a loathsome middle manager or heroically ripping off my outwear to reveal a chef's apron, but I suppose that is the effect of a vivid and somewhat unrealistic imagination. Apologies to all the middle managers and chefs out there.

The Organisation will also use this complex intermingling of your own identity and your job to their advantage. You see, if you were to simply view a job for what it is — a transaction of your time for their money — The Organisation's leverage is much reduced. If you don't feel you are receiving enough money in return for your time, then you move on to another place of employment that better aligns your perceived value with their willingness to pay for it. But when work becomes a part of your identity you become much more "sticky". You're less likely to leave over something as trivial as your pay, and besides, who would willingly walk out on "family" over an issue of a few dollars?

The other implication of your work becoming a key part of your identity relates to what happens when work is suddenly taken away from you. When you fail, or when a business is failing, the concept of good will is thrown out the door. You will quickly realise how expendable you are, and how naive you were to try and attach you own identity and personality to the entity that was paying you to deliver tasks that it had previously identified as being necessary. This was my own experience, whereby I had inadvertently aligned aspects of my own identity with my job, and when I was discarded I found myself with both a financial hole and a personality hole to fill. It caused more distress and angst than I am willing to admit.

It's not just true of a job. There are a myriad of people across the globe who make a single dimension of their extra-curricular activities the epicentre of their whole personality. By having personalised number plates and a matching custom paint job that heroes their favourite sports team, military experience, preferred dog breed or energy drink of choice, there are plenty of people who design their entire persona and presentation around one aspect of their consumer preferences.

Take a second to take stock of yourself. Are your clothes, conversations and decor all limited to one singular area of passion — be it work, a sporting team or a particular social issue? Are you one of those people who feels you have to broadcast a fairly narrow range of specific passions via your haircut, the decals on your car and your social media profile pics? Well, I have some news for you, and it's not good...

Work will overwhelm you with calls to invest much more of yourself into a job than simply turning up and doing what is asked of you. If you make the decision to integrate your job into your identity, or your identity into your job, you must be prepared to deal with the fallout when that aspect of your identity is taken away from you.

How to get ahead

ELSEWHERE IN THIS BOOK, I reference the fact that the workplace is most definitely NOT an egalitarian, meritocratic community. But it would be remiss of me not to talk about how you can ensure you get ahead in business. There are rules at play that — hopefully — you are becoming more aware of, and having this base knowledge is critical to determining how you are going to get ahead in the working world.

From wait staff to radiologists, tradespeople to middle managers, there are some general rules around the different paths you can take to achieve success at work, each with their own level of impact.

So, for anyone hoping to rise through the ranks, here's my unofficial but highly accurate ranking of how people actually get ahead in business — from least to most effective.

Being smart

The first, and least effective means of getting ahead? Being smart.

Being smart is, in fact, seen as an existential threat to everything that organisations and the people within them hold true. Being smart often leads to curiosity, questioning of the status quo, and a problem-solving mindset that is often focused entirely on creating objective solutions that challenge leadership, institutions and well-established inter-business norms. So obviously it's a really bad way of positioning yourself in a business.

Norms are normal, challenging them is not. Systems are like they are because they're what has been determined will work, not because there is a better way to do it.

Now don't get me wrong, objectively smart people can definitely get ahead in an organisation, but only when they combine those smarts with the other approaches outlined in the coming pages.

If your only talent is being smart, and you prioritise putting those smarts into identifying and calling out problems, and — God forbid — you propose solutions that are in conflict with the existing norms, then you are rapidly on your way to being recognised as a trouble-making, boat-rocking, stone in the shoe of anyone who has any authority. And that is a surefire way to limit your ability to get ahead in business, and most likely a fast path to be shown the door. So, let's put a pin in that idea.

Working hard

Not to be confused with being "busy", working hard is actually defined by doing work that in some way contributes to the success of the business (beyond merely having an overpopulated digital calendar), and creating empirical, measurable, meaningful and productive outcomes. This might mean you commit additional hours and discretionary effort into doing things for the business that deliver tangible and positive outcomes.

You may be asking yourself, "But how does working hard limit my ability to get ahead?"

There are several elements of hard work that are incredibly damaging to your own opportunities in an organisation. For one, no-one wants to lose a hard worker. When I say "no-one" I mean the people who manage you. By promoting someone who is a hard worker, management will recognise that they are immediately reducing the amount of work delivered by that individual, often to a far greater extent than if they were forced to replace a hard worker with someone who was not so hard working. So, by working hard and making a real difference you are often positioning yourself as un-promotable.

On top of this slightly awkward reality is the fact that no-one likes to work alongside someone who is a harder worker than them. Frankly you're making us all look bad and we're not here for that.

You'll find close peers and those on the same career trajectory will give you a fairly decent dose of stink eye if you out-work them, and their support may dry up when their livelihood, comfort or wellbeing (or a combination of all of these things) is being undermined and affected.

The other element of working hard is that hard workers inevitably attract more work. If you're outperforming those around you, you're not freeing up capacity to enjoy life; you're actually freeing up capacity for you to be the recipient of more work.

For instance if you're working in a box-making factory and you can produce 20 boxes every hour to Suzie's 10 boxes, you're not going home earlier or earning twice as much, you're just creating an assumption that you can do the job twice as well — and your boss is probably hoping to push that to 21 or 22 boxes an hour, or (if the consultants get involved) 30.

This remains true across all industries. Your hard work may not be rewarded with more downtime or higher responsibilities. You're actually much more likely to have more expectation heaped upon you in terms of your output, and you become a risk to overall productivity if you're promoted out of that box-making role and into a box-making-overseer role.

So scratch "being smart" and "working hard" off the list of most effective ways to get ahead.

Kissing ass

The third method of getting ahead is by being chummy with those who make decisions about who is being promoted.

Being a straight up brown nose/sycophant/boot licker/kiss ass (depending on your regional dialect) is a highly effective way of getting ahead. It's an undeniable human trait that people like to feel wanted and admired, and this human truth exists as strongly in the working world as it does in your own personal life. Having someone think like you, share the same opinion as you, and generally endorse anything you say is a highly effective means of quickly building rapport and camaraderie. And the larger the ego of the recipient, the more impactful this approach will be.

Managers of all ilks and persuasions have been falling for this one trick for millennia. A well-executed kiss-ass approach will have a rapid impact on your chances of promotion and increased responsibility (aka money). From goat herders to corporate high-flyers, the ability to make your boss love you because you make them feel good about themselves is almost impossible to replicate through any other means. And it's highly effective because it requires — by comparison — relatively little effort or genealogical luck to execute. Having said that, if you are blessed with intelligence and/or a hard-working approach as well as well-rounded lips and a complete lack of shame then you've hit the trifecta. And be advised you are unlikely to succeed in business with just hard work and/or smarts without having some level of ass-kissery involved. It is the one constant in business success.

So pucker up if you want to go up.

Being related

The final means of near-guaranteeing success is one that is most out of your control; being related to someone important. You will be shocked how many people have leveraged this as their best method of securing occupational advancement. Now I'm not saying that all people who are successful have relied on a close relationship to help facilitate that, but I am saying that their chances are materially and empirically improved by having someone they are related to making decisions about promotions and demotions. There are a raft of families and individuals who have seen enormous success because of their familial relationships, and you will inevitably come across people in business who share surnames or family trees with those much closer to the pinnacle of a business.

The interrelationship between these factors is obviously critical. The more of these things you have in your favour the more assured you are of professional success. It's simple to comprehend that being smart, working hard, kissing ass and being related to someone important offers you near infinitesimal advancement.

Remove any of these individual factors and you're going to see a gradual return to the mean.

Ask yourself: what is your method of getting ahead? And how can you optimise the mix to give yourself the best possible chance of reaching your own goals? If you're long on smarts but short on connections, it's clear where your priorities must lie if you want to climb the corporate ladder. Master this and the opportunities are immense.

PART 3
Navigating coworkers, bosses and bullshit

Luck is the biggest factor in your career

LIKE IT OR NOT, you are probably an incredibly lucky person on a global scale.

The fact you are here and able to read (or listen to) this book suggests that you are afforded some of the very luxuries of modern society.

You have been able to navigate your way digitally or physically to a bookstore, can afford to purchase this book, and have discretionary time and effort available to read it.

This relatively simple experience indicates that you're living a life whereby you have the means to earn money, transact that money for goods and services, have learnt how to read and comprehend language, and have the physical and mental safety to enjoy the consumption of the information in this book.

Now that may not seem very impressive to you, but as it happens, around half of the world's population doesn't even have access to clean water, so the idea of purchasing and reading a sort-of-management book is well outside the bounds of being a priority for many of those less fortunate. For something a little closer to home perhaps, it's also a published fact that around 54% of adults in the United States have literacy below a 6th grade level. So again, thank your lucky stars that by a global definition, you are lucky just to be able to pick up, read and comprehend this book. And have a glass of fresh water whilst doing it.

Of course, none of this means life doesn't suck sometimes. Privilege isn't a shield against suffering — but it is a multiplier of opportunity.

I consider myself incredibly privileged but that hasn't stopped me from wallowing in my own pity or despair as a result of decisions I may or may not have been involved in. There is tragedy happening at any given moment, to any given person, and the fact that someone out there might have it a little or a lot worse off doesn't make it any easier when you're doing it tough.

But on the balance of probabilities, we're probably up at the luckier end of the spectrum.

In the working world, luck is a significantly under-recognized factor in the success of any individual and we have to come to grips with that fact to avoid falling into a state of despair when things don't go our way.

There are a huge number of people you'll cross paths with — physically or digitally — who will try and convince you that their success is inextricably linked to their effort. They got there because of a better hustle, a more intense work ethic, greater intelligence or a superior ability to build connections.

Unfortunately, that's simply not true.

The truth is that they probably don't want to admit that they are where they are — maybe partly, but probably completely — because of luck and circumstance.

Ignoring for a second their geographical, social, genetic and socioeconomic luck, there's no doubt that during the course of their professional lives they've benefited from a huge amount of fortune. They applied for a job at just the right time. Their manager was promoted at just the right time. They were lucky enough to pick the business that didn't go into receivership, whose CFO wasn't skimming off the top, and whose business model wasn't fundamentally flawed. They sat in the right spot at lunch, had a drink with the right person at dinner, or just simply got lucky that the right person took a liking to them.

Every manager, every successful businessperson and every CEO has been the beneficiary of luck in some way. And the ones with any level of emotional and social awareness will happily acknowledge that fact. They're probably where they are because they're the people who have *most* benefited from luck. On the flip side, you could just as easily attribute someone's bad luck to being a leading cause for them struggling to make ends meet, or being homeless, or worse.

Successful people have often won a genetic, cultural, familial, socioeconomic and professional lottery. It's inevitable.

If you've struck out hard on any one or more of those things you've probably got a much tougher job ahead of you. That's just the facts.

And some people hate to admit that luck had anything to do with their success. It's somehow emasculating (or "defeminising") or embarrassing or undermines their own view of themselves.

From movie actors and elite sportspeople to CEOs and politicians, everyone has been — as Australians so brilliantly put it — kissed on the genitals by a fairy.

So why is this such a stark contradiction to those who so willingly broadcast their unflinching view that they are solely responsible for their own success? Well, how contradictory would it be to have curated this view of yourself amongst your peers, friends and professional network that you somehow got ahead because you were smarter and generally better than those around you, only to have to apportion some (or all) of that success on the simple rolling of a one hundred or one billion-sided dice? No rich person wants to suggest that they are rich because luck fell their way. No successful person wants to acknowledge that their success came from anything other than their own ability to pick themselves up by the bootstraps. It completely erodes the modern-day assumption that success in life is associated with merit and effort. Few successful people want to acknowledge that a large part of their success can be traced back to a sequence of fortunate events that were largely outside of their control.

As for me, I've certainly experienced my fair share of luck. From timely conversations to serendipitous reunions, it's all contributed to me being where I am today. As to whether that's created any form of "success"? Well, that's a completely different conversation.

Yes, there are certainly ways to skew the odds in your favour. If you work hard, learn, build relationships and make (generally) good decisions you can influence the likelihood of those sliding door moments that appear throughout your life. But don't mistake that for control. You're always just one conversation over lunch, one layoff, or one lottery ticket away from a completely different career.

Assholes and opinions

'Opinions are like assholes; everyone has one and they all stink.'

–Anonymous

Organisations have built themselves around whole structures that pre-determine which opinions and ideas are to be gleaned and listened to, and which should be ignored. Work, by its very nature, is the coming together of a diversity of people each with a variety of opinions. As a result, we must be intimately familiar with which are worth considering, whether ours is worth sharing, or whether they should all just be ignored.

Beyond the above quote being highly confronting and somewhat off putting as a visual, this proverb is almost always said with the express intent to devalue the opinions of others, and to promote the opinion of the orator. You will find this expression is often wheeled out by narcissists who have no intention of even considering for a moment that their opinion may, in fact, be wrong. The reality, of course, is that their opinion, like their asshole, could well be stinky too. And so it is for my own opinions.

Let's put to bed the idea that opinions — given their widespread availability — should be ignored out of hand. In fact, the word "opinion" could easily be substituted for "idea" or "perspective", and it gives the whole adage a distinctly different feel and intent. In essence, the speaker is proposing that their ideas are better than yours, which from my perspective makes the idea of identifying the actual asshole in all this a little easier.

There will be a number of occasions where circumstances will suggest to you — directly or indirectly — that your opinion or idea is not welcome or is of lesser value than those shared by the people who have authority.

I can't begin to count the number of forums and discussions I have been part of where the airing of my opinion would be seen as both controversial and unwelcome — not because it was wrong or ill-informed, but simply because it was part of a discussion where I was not deemed credentialed enough to share my perspective or expert knowledge. The power dynamic in most meetings is such that there will be those who are licensed to share (those deemed to have unstinky assholes), and those who are there to listen (those with stinky assholes). That delineation is most likely based on seniority, with almost no observed correlation between the seniority of the contributor and the quality of the opinion or idea. Often the only redeeming feature of the ratified opinion is that it has been provided by a senior leader, with the actual quality of that opinion being a distant second in terms of its suitability as a solution.

So I guess what the adage suggests is true, any given opinion is just as likely to stink regardless of who it belongs to.

And what's up with just assuming that other people's perspectives are worth dismissing out of hand? Sure, they might not have the depth of knowledge, but sometimes the fact that someone is somewhat distanced from the problem can provide really critical opportunities for their perspective to add value.

In fact, I'd go so far as to say it's absolutely crucial to source opinions about most workplace issues from those who have no specific working knowledge or expertise of the matter at hand. They're often the best means of ensuring you don't get caught with your pants down (and stinky asshole out) when that idea turns into practical application.

For instance, I — within reason — can tell you whether I have eaten an awful meal or heard an awful song without being a chef or a multi-platinum Grammy winning artist. I can also tell you when my favourite football team is playing like shit, or whether a book is bad (gulp) or a movie is best avoided. I may not be a complete subject matter expert on the decision making and execution of the skills that bring those things to bear, but as someone on the receiving end of the meal, song, book, movie or sporting performance, and having seen other comparable examples of each, I do feel like I have an opinion that is worth considering.

The same can be said of management decisions. Despite their self-professed knowledge, expertise and intelligence, it's a pretty reasonable rule of thumb that about half the time managers make decisions, those decisions end up being bad. And more often than not, there's someone in the very same building as you who could've told them how bad a decision was that they were about to make.

Let's take an example of a bad movie. There are millions of dollars and thousands of people involved. There are decisions of all sorts of size, scale and impact that are made over the course of a year or several years of planning and development. There are writers, editors, producers and God knows who else involved in the creation of this movie. The team is full of experts who have crafted their skills over years of practical and theoretical learning. And at the end of all this money and thousands of hours of smart people earnestly working away, we have the same likelihood that the result will be John Travolta in *Battlefield Earth* as Marlon Brando in *Apocalypse Now*.

The same applies in the business world. Too often there's a belief that the complexity of decision making — the unseen forces at play, the countless variables, and the supposed intellect of those in charge — makes the opinions of those affected by those decisions irrelevant or easy to dismiss. But as it is for the movie, you don't have to be an expert to predict the outcome of bad decisions.

Now you may not have to be in the room for every conversation, and you may not have to know every single consideration, but you may have a strong sense of when your boss or boss's boss (or even the CEO) makes an outrageously egregious and downright fucking stupid decision. In fact, like my later chapter on cliff diving, you'll find that you will spend a disproportionate amount of time blindly executing plans that even a slightly above-average kindergartner would know are going to create all the requirements for an impressively stinky outcome.

The CEO is the last person you should ask

CEOs seem to be the richest source of intelligence for those who want to understand how organisations truly succeed or fail. Of course for those of us who have worked in the real world, it's abundantly clear that CEOs are actually the last people you should ask when it comes to understanding the realities of how an organisation truly lives and breathes.

The best and most realistic guidance you will get in business will not come from a manager who operates in the upper or highest echelons, but from those who make up the vast, operational keel of the business. The waitstaff and junior executives and customer service team leaders are the best source of business information insofar as it will have relevance to what you are actually going to be doing and dealing with on a regular basis. Leave CEOs to author and indulge in books about "Optimising Organisational Alignment: A Genius at Work" and speak more to those who can provide more practical insights like "Jaimie and Evan have no idea what they are doing and are best buddies with Peta so be careful what you say."

It reminds me of a personal story that cemented this perspective.

I went to school with a guy who became a CEO, but who otherwise gave every signal that he was a pretty normal human.

There is no doubt his work is demanding, that the decisions are challenging and the many interested stakeholders are mystifying (my words, not his). And from my experience of him outside of work, he has always been a great friend and person. A good family man, involved in his community, and a great person to spend time with having a drink or meal.

From a work perspective he has oversight of several thousand employees who are split between customer-facing roles and technical roles, and he has oversight of a number of facilities dotted throughout urban and regional centres across the country. And he's in charge of heaps of money.

So imagine my surprise when I realised that this otherwise astute, intelligent and socially conscious man had his eyes painted on when it comes to the realities of what those in his business, and many organisations like it, are actually dealing with on a daily basis.

For instance, we once had a conversation about those generations behind us, and the different ways in which they prefer to communicate. His position essentially boiled down to "outside of face-to-face, a phone call is the most effective way to communicate with someone". His experience was that so much of the ambiguity in the working world could be solved through a simple chat over the phone. Past histories are laid to rest, differences in opinion can be quickly resolved, the nuances of the written language are avoided, and there's a human connection that can't be replicated in any other form of digital communication. He acknowledged that face-to-face was the premier way to resolve business issues, but in the absence of that, a phone call would soon put agitated minds to rest.

He was therefore somewhat taken aback when I told him that all of his assumptions were misguided, and that in fact he was an idiot with no sense of the realities his team faced on a daily, or hourly basis (disclaimer: I had been partaking in his very kind, liquid-based hospitality up to this point).

My counter to his perspective was this: as the CEO it is perfectly reasonable to assume that people will most likely drop whatever they are doing to pick up the phone when he calls. His management team, with whom he probably spends the majority of this time, would not only repay that kindness, but would likely expect the same from those they call. In essence, he's largely operating in an echo chamber of people making calls to subordinates who are — through the power imbalance typical of large organisations — obliged to pick up the phone when they come calling.

But to the rest of us, from middle management to those on the tools, the likelihood is that our efforts would simply register as another missed call. So we resort to other more passive means of communicating, whether that is email, chat, smoke signal or messenger pigeon. And sure, on the very odd occasion that we might resort to a phone call, we're unlikely to expect or receive the level of consideration, empathy, politeness or responsiveness that we might receive were we the CEO of his company, or any company, making that same call.

My observation was that he, as CEO, was probably one of the most inappropriate people to provide guidance on how best to communicate, collaborate or simply work with those up and down the business hierarchy.

And yet we hear so much from CEOs about how best to operate and thrive within business. If his perspective on phone calls was so disconnected from the real-life experience of the majority of those who go to the mines each day, then what is the likelihood that he can provide guidance about dealing with troublesome colleagues, business inefficiencies and management incompetence?

So that's where my perspectives and observations come from. No CEO, and very few of my colleagues, actively pick up the phone should I call. None of them are waiting patiently for my perspective or inputs, and fewer still give any time of day to worrying about what I may be thinking or trying to achieve. For that reason, my supposition is that CEOs and those in organisations of their ilk and influence are — by definition — completely detached from the realities of what happens in the swollen underbelly of business, and that they are therefore the last ones we should refer to in order to understand how we should operate in those same environments.

As for CEOs and upper management, their insights are limited to "voice of team" and "customer satisfaction" data, which is sanitised, aggregated and misrepresented by vested interests, and they don't have the level of interaction and honest conversations with everyday members of the team like most normal people would assume. They exist in a highly regulated and guarded environment, where information is only shared that is meant to a) appease them, b) appeal to them, c) reinforce what those around them want them to hear and/or d) position an issue in a way that serves the purposes of those presenting it.

And watch out if you feel the courage to present a counter view to the perspectives of the People Partner/CX Oracle/Strategy Mastermind (or any other manager for that matter) in any organisation. No-one is actually interested in the truth if it risks their ego, seniority, narrative or status.

If you are looking for practical wisdom on how to navigate your workplace you may be looking in the wrong direction. Stop listening to executives and start paying attention to the people who will be doing the work alongside you.

As for my friend, the CEO? I called him 22 times in a row from a hidden number and he didn't even pick up once. I should've emailed him.

Your boss probably isn't a leader

That's the short version.

The long version is a little more convoluted.

Let me start by asking you a simple question. Have you ever worked for someone who was roundly applauded by those above them, but they made your skin crawl and life hard? It's likely that they are an effective manager but lack the credentials to define themselves as a leader.

The reality is that the vast majority of managers are incapable of leadership (despite their LinkedIn profile summary), and most businesses are completely bare when it comes to leaders.

The key problem is that organisations are much more comfortable measuring practical outputs rather than messy concepts like likeability, camaraderie and vulnerability. Contemporary organisational culture rewards the ability to control, contain and report — traits that are associated with the concept of management. In contrast, leaders must show a willingness to serve those below them, as well as achieving the goals defined by those above them. Management only requires the satisfaction of those above, and largely ignores the needs of those below unless it impacts on the delivery of the tasks demanded of them.

Whilst the terms manager and leader may be interchangeable in a business context, there is a stark difference between the lived experience for those who work under each. There is also a near polar opposite philosophical approach as to how we should determine the effectiveness or ineffectiveness of a manager versus a leader.

For instance, the term "manager" evokes an image of someone who is responsible for controlling or organising a range of people, projects and processes. Managers are basically in charge of the human and non-human resources. Managing is a clinical term to describe moving things around to most effectively deliver on the task or tasks assigned to that manager. As a result, the concept of management does away with any pretences related to the humanity of the task at hand. You manage a budget or the cleaning of the house. You manage the serving of food. Those things require less mobilisation and enthusiasm of the participants but are tasks and chores that require completion. Therefore, the focus is on the task at hand rather than any effort to build camaraderie or enthusiasm for the task. An objective is defined, it's turned into a range of tasks, and it must be completed. I would posit that all businesses require processes managed, and therefore it requires the skills of a manager to coordinate the implementation and completion of those processes to complete the task.

As the above definition clearly outlines, it's completely removed from humanity. People become assets moved around the whiteboard, much like other resources, such as money and time. Some managers might be human and display some level of emotional intelligence, but it's not an absolute requirement.

Leadership, however, evokes a very different image. The term elicits images of great sportspeople or coaches motivating their players on the sideline and creating a sense of team and interdependency. It conjures an image of military leaders of all eras rallying their troops and their country, overcoming seemingly impossible odds, and celebrating alongside their charges when success or survival is assured. It's Tom Hanks in Saving Private Ryan essentially. Putting others first, recognising the need to acknowledge and nurture the humanity in those they oversee, and being willing to sacrifice themselves in some way in order to improve the chances of those around them seeing success. This image also talks to honesty, a willingness to call out bad behaviour when it jeopardises the success of the wider team, and a readiness to self-sacrifice when duty demands it. Compassion, respect, sympathy and frankness. These are the ideals that come to mind when I think of a leader.

In short, if The Organisation is using a single methodology built around management input to measure the effectiveness of managers and leaders then that business is fucked (and misinterpreting the concept of leadership). And if you can't tell the difference between management and leadership positions – like explicitly being able to articulate which roles require which – then things are doubly fucked.

Leadership is not a new concept. My favourite quote that captures the essence of leadership versus management is from the last century. It has been attributed to Antoine de Saint-Exupéry[15]:

> *"If you want to build a ship, don't drum up the men to gather wood, divide the work, and give orders. Instead, teach them to yearn for the vast and endless sea."*

Management is the drumming up of people to gather wood. Leadership is about teaching those same people to yearn for the vast and endless sea. That is leadership and motivation — to create a longing for something larger and more impactful to give today's tasks a greater meaning.

Now let's take a look at who is best placed to determine the effectiveness of a "leader" over a "manager".

For a manager, it's relatively simple. They are assigned a task by those in authority, and their success is determined by the completion or otherwise of that task. Upper management — as a proxy for those who assign tasks — are best able to determine if the manager was able to manage things to completion using the resources as effectively as possible.

A leader, however, asks very different questions as to who is best

---

15   I have always had an affinity with this quote and was quite disillusioned that in doing research for this book it appears that Antoine de Saint-Exupéry may not have explicitly said these words. However, for the purposes of simplicity I have attributed this quote to him. It also remains a mystery as to how de Saint-Exupéry died, although it is assumed that his aircraft crashed on a reconnaissance mission during World War 2. He was probably sent out on a mission by his manager.

to determine if they have been effective. Of course a leader who can't complete the tasks assigned to them could be argued to be ineffective. Let's assume for a moment that they can lead a team into completing a task as defined by those empowered to define the task. This sounds very similar to the idea of measuring the effectiveness of a manager. Has this person used the resources effectively to complete the task? There is no need to measure motivation or enthusiasm or "feel-good-vibes". Those who have ordained a task necessary can therefore determine whether that task is complete and therefore whether that manager has been effective.

Leadership asks for much more. If we are to believe the definition I've shared of a leader as a person who needs to complete tasks but also do it in a way that considers the humanity of those they are charged to lead, then the means through which we measure "leadership" extends beyond simply completing the task.

The key difference between a manager and a leader is the role and reception of the *team* in completing the task.

So in order to judge leadership we must consult the team on whether leaders have been effective. The team must be a significant contributor, if not the final arbiter, as to whether a leader has indeed led. Is the task complete? If so, they have managed. Is the task complete and was the team engaged, enthused and empowered in the delivery of the task? They have led.

By this rationale, wouldn't it make sense for the team to provide the most critical feedback when it comes to measuring the effectiveness of a leader? And if this is the case, why the fuck do most organisations fail to involve the team in measuring the performance of said leader?

For those who have been in the working world for some time, you will be well aware that the determination of a good "leader" is almost exclusively made by those in authority with little to no attempt to understand the experience of the team who has been assigned to the delivery of a task. The real reason for this is that business is primarily made up of *managers*, and almost exclusively measures the effectiveness of people through the lens of management criteria. The term leader is often thrown around, but it is rarely actively measured if we are to assume that consultation with the team on the performance of a leader is a key measure.

It's reasonable to ask yourself why "leaders" in business don't rely on — in some way — the perspectives of who they lead in determining how good a leader they are.

The answer is simple. Doing this would fundamentally tip the intentionally designed power imbalance that exists between the team and the senior leader.

The power and authority of those more senior than you is designed and developed with the concept of "management" in mind. Any leadership credentials are superfluous to this fact. If, all of a sudden, you had the ability to determine the effectiveness of those more senior than you — and therefore influence the potential for them to progress in the business — they would've handed over some of their power to you. And that's not something they are willing to do. It's far easier to impress someone above them — over whom they have no power — through the deeds of those they manage. To suddenly include genuine leadership credentials in those discussions becomes messy, complex and a lot of hard work.

You will hear the terms "leader" and "leadership" bandied around in business. But the truth of the matter is that those terms are performatory only. In all my years of reporting to supposed "leaders" I have never once been consulted on the performance of those who are leading. Nor have I ever been in an environment whereby those that are supposedly being led are consulted on the performance of leaders. That's left to their peers and — more often — their managers.

Becoming a leader takes time, coaching, mentoring and relationship building. It's so much easier to just be judged on what you got done rather than how you did it. That's measurable, tangible and binary. Leadership is not. And besides, who wants their underlings to impact on their management aspirations for the future?

So don't be fooled. You will come across a range of managers and will find managers use the term leadership a lot, but it will only be on very rare occasions that you will actually find yourself working for a leader. Some people might argue they've never worked for anyone but managers. So next time you find yourself working for someone who proclaims to be a leader, ask yourself whether you are truly being led.

The best person at the job may not be the best person for the job

THERE IS A MISGUIDED assumption that the people who are good at one particular work task will naturally be good at any other tasks assigned to them. This is most obvious when a technical expert is promoted to a management role.

The Peter Principle goes some way to explaining how this circumstance comes about[16].

In essence, the theory is that in any hierarchical structure, individuals will be promoted until they reach a level where their skills no longer align with the requirements of the role. In essence, they are unable to perform their duties effectively given they have been promoted due to their current skills and performance, rather than the skills required to succeed in their new, higher-level role.

It can be boiled down to this simple premise: being good at their job does not mean that someone will be good at managing others who are doing the job. There are multiple examples of the flawed assumption that technical experts would make great leaders, but perhaps the most familiar example is on the sporting field. There are innumerable instances where great players have been asked to be coaches, and the sporting history books are littered with examples of where this has led to angst, anger and inevitable failure. That hasn't stopped the working world from persisting with it though.

It's always struck me as odd that the police and military forces are only ever run by career police officers and military personnel. They've generally worked their way up the ranks, played the

---

16   The Peter Principle was defined by Laurence J Peter, so it's not intended to be a slight on any managers who have the name Peter, although that's not to say they are immune from falling victim to the incompetence that is a hallmark of the theory.

politics somewhat effectively, created the right allies, and maybe overseen a controversy or two, but they've ultimately climbed up the ladder to be the public face of their chosen military industrial complex.

It seems such a contrast to just about every other large private or public organisation.

Can you imagine the complete state of chaos if your multi-billion-dollar supermarket chain would only consider night-fill staff or cashiers for the top job? Or if the CEO of Nike was just the fastest runner or the best passer or the biggest dunker? Take nothing away from people who are doing the hard yards — but let's all agree that there are much more rounded sets of requirements to lead a vast and complex business.

What about if your friendly neighbourhood multi-billion-dollar fossil fuel mining company was led by Damo, the greatest long-haul truck driver the world has ever seen?

The best shelf stacker isn't the best at running supermarkets, the best runner isn't running Nike, and the best load hauler isn't leading that mining conglomerate, so why does the "best" police officer run the police?

It's an oddity that I can't quite explain.

I would presume that being the most senior manager of a large, complex entity would require a range of skills that isn't limited to those who show some level of expertise in the technical aspects of their chosen career.

Let's persist with the police force as an example. With administrators and investigators, information technologists and psychologists, safety advisors and community partners, the assumption is that it would require a deep knowledge of highly complex organisational design with far reaching governance and influence requirements. It may be fair, then, to suggest that those requirements might naturally rule out someone who's entire professional experience was limited to policing.

Perhaps the overwhelming positive perception of police forces in creating confidence amongst the people they serve, and generally remaining controversy free from a cultural and financial perspective, puts my cynical brain and natural organisational curiosity to rest. It might even go so far as to act as a counter argument to the fact that the best practitioner may not be the best leader. Or maybe not. I guess that police forces don't have to make money so that takes a lot of pressure off individuals in leadership positions. No shareholders, no voting against your remuneration, no public scrutiny of your profit and loss statement. Must be nice...

So be warned when you are working in a business whereby the best technician is suddenly elevated to the role of manager. The best doctor should not run the hospital, the best accountant should not run the accounting firm, and the best member of the waitstaff does not necessarily have the skills to run the whole front of house and kitchen. Leadership is a skill unto itself and is often a completely different capability when compared to technical expertise. Technical capability and leadership capability should therefore be viewed through quite separate lenses.

It also means you can't presume that the colour blind and one-eyed designer might not become the best Chief Marketing Officer you've ever seen, or that Clumsy Colin might not be a real force when it comes to leading the front of house and pulling the kitchen crew into line.

In fact, if you hear a manager referencing their own technical skills in their day-to-day interactions, chances are they are shit at managing people and teams, and have to resort to that one area of egotistical safety through which to assert their dominance. If questions about management decisions are answered with responses focused on the technical skills of the manager in question, that's a sign that this individual lacks some of the core requirements of management (and probably a sense of self-awareness as well).

So we must reflect on our abilities when we are looking at promotion. Are we the best technical expert? Or are we a technical expert with leadership capabilities? If the answer to the first question is "yes", and the answer to the second is "no", then it's likely that we don't yet have the required skills to take on a management role.

Now there's no problem with being an absolute technical expert with no ability or inclination to manage people. That's a fine path to follow and one that will probably offer significant upside whilst reducing the distress that comes with lacking management expertise.

If you do have management (or even leadership) aspirations, then it's critical to realise that there are specific skills required to effectively do that job over and above simply being good at it. It's also a great way to avoid the risk of falling victim to The Peter Principle.

Anyway, signing off to go and apply for a job in the police force. The absence of commercial, performance, cultural and social accountability quite appeals to me.

The Law of Individual Excellence

THE LAW OF INDIVIDUAL EXCELLENCE: *The belief that you are better than others at your job, which justifies your promotion. Once promoted, this belief resets — you're now the best at this new job. Repeat until retirement or board appointment.*

Management by its nature requires an ego.

To be a manager you need to convince yourself that you would make a good manager. You therefore assume you are amongst the best when it comes to the task of managing, then leverage that assumption to assume that you are the most suitable person to be promoted to the next level of management in the business. Then after a while at that level, you assume you're the best (or even a little *too* good) at that job and therefore you assume that you should be promoted to the next level of seniority and so-on and so-forth until you assume you are the best CEO, in which case you then retire and join a board and naturally assume that you are better than any CEO as a result.

The Law of Individual Excellence fundamentally requires that the person in question considers themselves excellent at their job. So it stands that an individual is always assuming that they are better (or more individually excellent) than those below them, and reasonably better (and therefore more individually excellent) than those around them (and probably above them).

This is overwhelmingly the most common path that people take into management positions, and the concept of the "reluctant leader" is one best saved for movies and historical rewrites.

Of course, people don't operate in a vacuum. Therefore we are surrounded in the workplace by lots of people thinking they're better than everyone else in their orbit.

So what does that mean in practice?

Darwinism (if you believe in it) suggests that only those who are the best at surviving and thriving within an organisation will continue to scratch, claw and outlast those around them as they move up the organisational ladder. Ultimately you end up with this distilling of people who think they're pretty individually excellent *and* who have proven they are the most proficient at the cut and thrust of management, all slowly floating towards the top of any given organisation.

And you wondered why it's so dog-eat-dog up there.

Now what happens if something goes wrong? You've got a group of people who are personally determined — based on the Law of Individual Excellence — that they are better than those around them. In the case of a crisis, those same people have to reconcile themselves with the fact that things have gone wrong at the very moment where they have some level of responsibility for said thing going wrong.

So — given the Law of Individual Excellence — the last thing those in charge want to do is burst this illusion they have that they are better than those around them at whatever they do (a necessary feature of the Law of Individual Excellence). And they're surrounded by people who also want to avoid acknowledging that they may have fucked something up too because they are all of a similar view that they are more individually excellent that those around them. So, all of these people have a vested interest in ignoring the fact that something is going wrong, and maintaining the facade — alongside their peers — that things in fact have not gone wrong and that they remain better than those around them. Thus, they have protected the Law of Individual Excellence right across the organisation. Quite a paradox isn't it?.

If these same people actually have to resolve the fact something has gone wrong — normally pointed out to them by someone above them who has correspondingly convinced themselves that they are better than those around them per the Law of Individual Excellence — they can't possibly acknowledge that they were anything but the most excellent at their job so need to protect themselves as much as possible from the reality which suggests they may in fact not be as good as those around them. That would be in direct contradiction with the Law of Individual Excellence (i.e. that they might not be the most excellent individual and therefore might not be worthy of that next sought-after promotion).

If this sounds confusing — and it should — it gives a very basic glimpse into what happens when things fuck up and everyone else thinks it has to do with the incompetence of others. The whole system becomes a stirred-up ants' nest of people trying desperately to avoid others identifying the fact that it's them who may have fucked up.

The major issue is that those below them (who probably also think they are more excellent than those above them) now know that those above them have fucked something up. So those above them try and limit awareness around them that they have fucked up, whilst those below them can see that they've fucked up. Again, the Law of Individual Excellence requires — nay demands — that those higher up must believe that they are better and more excellent at their job than those below them. A serious fuck-up on their watch would be a complete contradiction to this much important fact and therefore must be dismissed out of hand.

Quite a mess, isn't it? Does this ring true for your own experience? Well hang on for a little longer because we've nearly gone full circle.

Deep breath.

So now you have those below them (who think they're more excellent) thinking that those above them (who think *they're* more excellent) have fucked up, and those above them (who think *they're* more excellent) not wanting those below them (who think *they're* more excellent) knowing that they know they fucked up.

So now you have people working on unfucking things without wanting those above (and below) to know they've fucked up, whilst those below (and above) *know* they've fucked up.

It's exhausting, but it's the reality of the business world.

You've undoubtedly seen this play out in multiple ways through your own experience. It may come in the form of blame shifting. It might appear as finger pointing. It might even appear as blame pointing and finger shifting. And in the worst case, you'll find that it's business-as-usual given no one is willing to stick their neck out to suggest that they or anyone else is even marginally responsible for the fuck up.

This also explains why people are so vehemently against having those below them point out that they may not be as excellent as they assume they are. It totally rocks the fundamentals of the Law of Individual Excellence (which requires that the individual assume they are the most individually excellent) because it means that their assumptions may not be correct. That would be a realisation that would break the laws of the physical and theoretical world in their mind (and the Law of Individual Excellence more specifically) upon which their whole professional persona is based.

Sometimes on very rare occasions these same people might even commit a small amount of their time to trying to unfuck things, although that's not necessarily the case. Now throw into this the fact that a fuck up normally involves a number of people or teams right up and down a business, and you have people in a near state of paralysis staring into the void or outright denying that anything is fucked up.

The short version is that no one could possibly be responsible for the fuck up, that it's inevitably someone else's fuck-up, and the whole thing is a total fuck-up right up and down the system.

So don't point out to managers that they fucked up. The Law of Individual Excellence would require that they deny it anyway.

Being aware of the Law of Excellence offers you a very unique opportunity to understand the key driver for many of the people around you. Firstly, they are likely of the view that they are somewhat better than just about everyone else at their job, and secondly, this very fact means that they're unlikely to acknowledge that they could ever be anything but excellent at their job. Your own survival may rely on acknowledging and navigating this very premise, and it gives you some idea of why no-one is seemingly out to improve things that are so obviously fucked up.

Corporate cliff diving

"WELL WOULD YOU jump off a cliff if Frankie told you to?"

We've probably all heard a version of this riposte from our parents or guardians at some stage in our childhood. Often, it's when we've been co-opted by a friend (not always Frankie, but someone much like Frankie) into rationalising stupid behaviour of one kind or another.

"Frankie told me to drink it!"

"Frankie said we should light it on fire!"

In essence, we're explaining away our own ill-considered actions by pointing to the fact that a third party had proposed it, and — most importantly — it resulted in us being chastised by those in authority for naively following that proposed course of action. Would you go so far as to jump off a cliff if someone suggested it? Of course not.

Common sense and self-preservation would prevent you from doing something catastrophic, and therefore you should try and apply some critical thinking to doing that dumb thing, even if Frankie suggests you do it. It might not involve a cliff this time, but it's a clear warning that you should stop and think carefully before blindly following someone else's guidance just in case you end up in a bloody heap at the bottom of a crevasse somewhere.

The lesson our guardians were trying to instill was for us to think for ourselves, and apply commonsense to our decision-making rather than simply adhering to the suggestion (or explicit instruction) from someone else.

It's important to recognise that our parents had positive intentions when they told you not to unquestioningly follow your friend's advice. They were trying to embed a critical message about self-preservation in your formative years. And it's safe to assume that many of us saw it as advice that would serve us well throughout our life; namely to think first, act second, and to be careful of external forces telling you what to do because it could end in tragedy.

Well, you should ignore this very sage and reasonable advice once you walk into the working world.

Work will regularly ask you to dismiss the idea of self-preservation or individual agency under the auspices of doing what's right for The Organisation. There is an illusion — fostered by much of the rhetoric around business — that you are somehow responsible and entirely accountable for whatever course of action you might take.

Work will likely give you a crash course in cliff diving. You see, you are far more likely to be asked to jump off metaphorical cliffs in the work environment than your parents ever foresaw or were willing to admit. In the working world, Frankie isn't just that irresponsible and naive kid, Frankie might well be your boss, and, as your boss, Frankie will not only be telling you to jump off cliffs, but he or she will be defining the height, trajectory and speed at which you need to jump off that cliff. And then they'll review that cliff jump in a follow up meeting to determine if you've carried out the dive in a way that aligns with their expectations and delivers on organisational cliff diving needs.

So how do we find ourselves in a position where organisations are invariably pushing themselves and their team towards the edge of the cliff?

More often than not businesses fail in the "critical thinking" component of analysing whether a particular action is a good one or not. Internal and external pressures often mean that any attempts to critically assess a particular course of action have happened in closed rooms involving people who are probably being paid much more than you, who are dealing with internal and external forces that are unknown to you, and who have created a decision to head down one particular path that may indeed be counterproductive or absurd. Like jumping off a cliff for instance.

This is the concept of corporate cliff-diving. You have signed over your own individual agency, and instead become one of those following the lead lemming off a cliff.

My experience in large organisations is that you will be given some level of agency, but only insofar as it delivers on the very explicit requirements of those in positions of authority. We are assigned clear tasks with narrow margins that limit individual thought or execution and are given some illusion of choice that will only have a minor and almost incalculable impact on the final outcome.

The more common experience is that you are told to do something, and our success is measured on how closely we can carry out that task when compared to the expectations of those above us. Success is rarely defined by the level of innovation brought to bear in order to achieve an outcome. It's more commonly measured based on our willingness to fulfil our obligation with as little variation as possible from the approach prescribed to us.

So what happens in this scenario when almost all individual agency is removed from the individual assigned a given task?

The first implication of demanding people follow direction unquestioningly is a removal of initiative and innovation in a business or team. If no-one is rewarded for critically assessing a path forward and being able to make amendments based on their best judgement, then why would they try time and time again? Individual efforts to contribute will be eroded, and the likelihood of coming up with new and inventive ways to do things will soon disappear.

The second implication goes beyond how individuals might tackle a particular task, and into their mindset when performing that task. By removing the incentive for people to use their own initiative to solve a problem, managers are correspondingly making individuals complicit in executing a solution that they have no investment in. Whether that solution is good or bad, the removal of an individual's ability to influence the solution removes any psychological safety they may have felt. Their internal narrative might soon take a decidedly ominous turn.

It's reasonable to ask yourself, should you find yourself in this position, how necessary are you to an organisation if your unique ability to solve challenges and provide ideas are superseded by mandates from those above you? Your personal investment and capabilities in the delivery of a task are removed, and instead you become a tool that executes tasks as defined by others. You become inherently replaceable because you have no impact on the task other than seeing that it is done. In fact, you may be increasing your own risk of replacement because you're actively better at coming up with solutions than others who might be most effective at simply delivering a pre-defined solution. Namely, you'll be measured on your ability to lead the team towards the cliff, rather than your ability to find another path to your destination.

By the time that direction is cascaded down to you there is no authentic opportunity for you to critically assess and remedy the proposed course of action.

And further to that, your whole success at work may be explicitly linked to your willingness to take that mandated leap into thin air.

The business world is full of Frankies, and you may need to get comfortable with taking a few death-defying leaps, despite what your parents told you all those years ago.

Be friendly but be careful who you befriend

THERE IS A COMMON misnomer that work is a place to make friends. Whilst nice in theory, in practice the concept of making friends in the workplace is fraught with danger and conflicting needs. A better approach is to recognise that the workplace is a place to be friendly, rather than a place to befriend.

Let us unpack that for a moment.

If the hypothesis is that you can't truly be friends with people in the workplace then let's look at the factors that support that argument.

First, we must define the key elements of friendship. Friendships are built on a mutual affection between people. This mutual affection has hallmarks such as trust, honesty, support and loyalty, and also calls for the offering of emotional and practical assistance in times of need. Most importantly, friendship must be voluntary and built on respect and acceptance. We must be able to confide in each other without fear of betrayal, and that confidence is built on honest and open communication.

So let's consider why many of these things are incompatible with work.

Why managers can't be friends

Firstly, let's take your direct manager out of the equation.

The relationship between you and your manager is necessarily defined by a power imbalance through the manager/subordinate relationship. In its simplest terms, they have the power to fire you, and you do not have the power to fire them. In the working environment this fact is probably the most extreme version of any potential outcomes of your relationship.

The reality is that your manager is probably going to fire you and one hundred of your peers before they put themselves on the chopping block. Given they are in a position of power, that imbalance automatically means that any interactions with your manager are skewed. Only one of you has the means to fire the other, and would likely do so if required, so that makes any mutual benefit and honesty (key pillars of positive friendships) impossible. And this rule applies to anyone who has the ability to determine your fate and future prospects in your organisation of choice.

Friendships are built on a number of factors, but the requirement for honesty, trust and vulnerability are core to any true friendship. Those things are incompatible with a professional working environment. Professionalism and vulnerability are at odds with each other despite what modern day leadership books might tell you. Vulnerability and honesty are impossible in most working environments given the need for the protection of business critical information, such as whether you are going to get fired.

This won't stop managers and HR from trying to embed the concept of brutal honesty and the idea of being a family into your working relationships. We are under constant pressure to try and forge relationships with those around us under the auspices of "friendship", but the reality is that no friend is going to fire you when their budget starts looking questionable, and managers would probably get rid of you if you shared some of your true feelings in the same way you might with a friend.

So the manager/subordinate relationship falls short on a number of the key factors that facilitate being true friends. Namely honesty, mutual benefit, acceptance and open communication.

Why peers can't be friends

It seems completely reasonable — with the removal of the power imbalance that exists between managers and subordinates —

that you could put in place a mutually beneficial relationship that skirts closer to the concept of friendship with those you regularly work alongside.

The reality is that the competitive hunt for resources and opportunity will create a barrier between you and them.

What happens when you are pitted against each other for promotion, demotion or removal? How would that impact any normal friendship? And what would happen if you were pitted against each other for scarce resources such as humans, money or management attention? Those fundamental frictions — whilst not always constant — are likely to appear in any organisation and undermine the concept of true, unabashed friendship. These are not just hypotheticals; they are the realities of the working world where there is a constant battle for the resources that make doing your job feasible. Ironically, I curl my toes at the thought of considering my workmates family, but there are some key similarities. You can't choose your workmates, and often the interpersonal relationships are driven by greed, distrust and a need to appease those who lead the team. So I guess your colleagues are like family in that regard.

The peer relationship as a friendship is again skewered by the circumstances into which you are thrust in a business setting. The pursuit for resources means that there is a proclivity to try and secure those resources in any way possible, and this undermines values such as mutual respect, open communication and selflessness.

Why subordinates can't be friends

The dynamic between you and your subordinates is obviously the inverse of that between you and your manager, so the risks and limitations seem obvious. But let's lay them out anyway in the spirit of being comprehensive.

Whilst a subordinate may not be so frank as to articulate their feelings towards you, it's inevitable that there is an almost insurmountable barrier to friendship that exists between you and them. Namely, the fact that you may have to fire them at some stage in the future.

Now that's a very big elephant sitting in the corner of any formal or informal setting where you might find yourself building rapport and common ground. Regardless of how likely it is that you may have to make them redundant, it's an undeniable fact that it will limit candour and vulnerability.

As a manager you are being paid to further the ambitions of the organisation, and your subordinates are a means through which you achieve those ambitions. Therefore, your subordinates are required to play their part. Anything counter to that creates a rift in your own commonalities, and that's a significant hurdle to honesty for both parties. Unless of course neither of you give a fuck about the ambitions of the business — in which case, you may have actually found yourself a new buddy.

How to make friends

So, if I've warned you off making friends with peers, managers and subordinates, then who does that leave? The honest truth is that you will establish friendships in the work environment, but it will require the mutual removal of several of the institutionalised limitations that exist in most organisations. If the conditions are just right, and the participants share the same values, then friendships most certainly do materialise, but it will only happen despite what the working world throws up at you.

Firstly, you will have to remove or reduce the factors at work that limit your ability to move towards friendship. This would mean the removal of a manager/subordinate dynamic, or the removal of the competition for limited resources. This is the simplest path to finding friends at work. There will be occasions where you are thrown into cross-functional groups or into wider teams where you interact with peers but don't overlap in responsibilities and therefore the conditions for friendship are much more fertile.

There are also certain scenarios that will present themselves where it's feasible to become friends with those who are subordinates and peers. I alluded to this concept earlier when I mentioned that it requires a mutual level of not-giving-a-fuck.

That doesn't necessarily mean that you don't care for the business and its objectives, but rather that you have removed any care about the business-preferred power dynamics between you and your subordinates or managers, or removed the competitiveness ordinarily required to achieve success over your peers.

From my experience, this actually offers the most opportunity for friendship. This requires the prioritisation of honesty and vulnerability over the dynamics imposed on you by business and is a quick means to recognise aligned values with those around you.

If you throw out the rule books around how relationships are supposed to work in a working context, you actually create the strongest relationships inside and outside of the working environment.

In essence, if neither of you has power over the other through agreement or organisational design, then there's a chance you could become chums.

What about making friends with those you used to work with? Well, with the removal of the constraints and conflicts that are typical of organisations, there is the potential that you can evolve from being friendly into being friends. Those relationships will most likely blossom once you are freed from the yoke of the competitiveness and preferential treatment that is so typical of any workplace.

And if you were friends before you became colleagues? Well let's just hope that your shared friendship and values are robust enough to handle whatever work will put in your way.

Life is a group assignment

Most of us have experienced the sense of dread that the idea of a group assignment evoked when we were at school, college, or anywhere else.

I remember my abject horror when the words "group assignment" were uttered in my years as a student. Being thrust into a team of randomly selected people whose only similarity was that we were in the same class doing the same subject at the same time seemed ominous and overwhelming.

You would find yourself in a position where your personal success was intrinsically linked to this haphazard group of individuals (yourself included) who must all now contribute to creating something extraordinary. Or at least passable.

Well, it turns out the working world is one big group assignment.

Work will require you to get intimately comfortable with the fact that your own progress and success is almost entirely reliant on your fellow misfits. You must learn their ways, their nuances, their strengths and "opportunities" (i.e. faults), and you must do all of this in the midst of trying to deliver something that approaches a competent outcome.

I'm actually an advocate of group assignments, particularly those that put you together with as diverse a group of people as possible. None of this pick-your-buddies stuff. You want a combination of the meek, the mental and the meticulous. You want the odd-one-out and the "yes" man or woman, the pacifist and self-promoter. You want the dim-witted and the quick-witted. The greatest diversity, across the largest number of measures possible, the better.

So let's take a look at how you ended up here. You were propelled into this role by some unknown force (probably your parents initially), and through a series of inexplicable events you find yourselves in the same business, on the same team, and at the same time. Now you have to come together and make the complex dynamics work in order to achieve an assigned objective. The reality is that in those heady and carefree days of being a student the requirements of any group assignment were often specific and concise. That's in contrast to the group assignments out in the working world which are likely less well defined, and the marking process is much more ambiguous. There's no such thing as High Distinctions, GPAs and Honours out here. The corporate world is much more binary. There's success or not, and it's often only decided at completion what the marking system is.

You see, group projects in an educational environment will prepare you for the competence and incompetence of others upon which you must rely in the working environment. People will let you down, not show up, plagiarise, lie and steal. They'll also shock you with their contribution, astonish you with their intelligence, and leave you dumbstruck with their insight.

Being thrust into a group of relatively randomly selected individuals will also offer something that can't be gleaned from sticking with the familiar. You will come across a broad range of personalities that often offers the greatest opportunity for learning and the ability to expand your own horizons. It will also teach you about patience, resilience and reliability. It will also help you understand more about yourself.

But there remain some inalienable truths that are common to anyone who has been part of almost any group. And that is the appearance of some very particular personas. This remains true for almost every team you will find yourself leading or contributing to in a work context.

I've tried to capture the almost inevitable cross section of identities you will come across in a group setting. It's not exhaustive, but it will provide some insights that may help hone your own approach and identify what role you might play in achieving success in any group project.

The Organiser

Fundamental to the success of any group, this person will be the first to recognise that no group can succeed without some level of coordinated order. They will probably start the group chat, begin the process of assigning tasks, and might even take on some of the leadership requirements in order to get the task completed. They're definitely going to issue the "skeleton" version of the slide deck or document to help get the ball rolling.

They are necessary and will likely act as the catalyst for action and outcome. They can also be a bit of a control freak, and can often start falling apart as deadlines, tasks and responsibilities start to slip. Without someone in this role the chances of success get closer to zero.

The Ghost

In their mind meetings are optional, contributions are flexible and having their name on the final outcome is inevitable. In some instances, they can be the senior representative in the group who through "busyness" or rhetoric about other priorities will find their way out of actually contributing anything. But that won't stop them from ensuring they are represented in all sessions with senior leaders given their need for acknowledgement and recognition, and they can often become great promoters of the work once it is complete, albeit with very little contribution to the actual work itself.

It's often a surprise to some outsiders when a Ghost's name appears as a contributor. Sure, they may have been on the meeting invite list, but does anyone remember them actually turning up to any of the discussions we had?

Ghosts quite often evolve into "Hijackers" once things are nearing completion and often focus their communications on The Organiser in order to remain abreast of progress without having to commit any time and effort. This is also helpful in giving them enough intel to project a perception of involvement to others.

The Hijacker

They often initially blend into the crowd à la The Ghost, but soon make their presence known once a project matures to the point where it requires visibility across influential audiences. They begin by intentionally remaining anonymous amongst the crowd but make a dramatic appearance once things start to escalate and are nearing completion.

Their goal is recognition, and they will happily steamroll over the top of other team members when they see an opportunity to leverage the project for their own promotional needs.

During later stages of a project, they become very vocal – especially in the context of who should be presenting what to important stakeholders. They also rely on The Organiser to ensure they are present in key forums where work is being shared with influential decision makers. Don't be surprised if they take to LinkedIn to reiterate how fundamental they have been to the delivery of the work, even if they're not sure of who contributed what. Sometimes they might even learn the names of those who they have been working alongside, although this is not always the case.

The Silent Assassin

Silent but deadly, they'll creep around the background in the manner of The Ghost, but they will contribute far more than anyone could fully predict. They'll go from villain to hero when they share that initiative-defining contribution or will come to the fore in the final frenetic moments of the project. They are unassuming but deeply necessary. They're lowkey and unlikely to listen to direction, but they'll offer a moment of killer inspiration or unmatchable contribution when things seem lost.

The Suckerfish

They will feed on the morsels left behind by others in the group but will never source sustenance of their own volition.

Incapable of individual thought, they are best identified by their neediness. They are conscientious but occasionally clueless, and panic is their standard state of mind. They require hand holding, clear guidance, and an unquenchable need to be calmed as the pressure and timelines start building up.

Seemingly small issues can rapidly become big ones, and they can be distracted by anything remotely irrelevant. They occasionally morph into a fantastic Organiser given their need for visibility on progress and an appetite to focus on the measurable for relief. They can be naive to the (lack of) presence of Ghosts and are dismayed when Silent Assassins seemingly drop their signature game-changing contribution out of nowhere.

They'll sweat the small stuff, generally turn up the pressure gauge across the team, and will be overwhelmed with relief once things are over.

The Swiss Army Knife

Mr, Mrs or Ms Fix-it, they fill in inevitable voids left through the absence and distraction of other team members. They plug holes across the board, and whilst they might not have deep experience their ability to adapt to the changing needs and circumstances of the group makes them vital. They have a "can do" attitude, and their enthusiasm is often fuelled through exasperation at what is not being done.

They appreciate completion and competence and are a critical cog in the successful delivery of any team project. From booking venues to creating the final draft of that mind blowing presentation (all important in the working world), they're a fundamental ally for Organisers and the engine room when it comes to tangible outcomes and actual delivery.

The "Perfect" Team

Unsurprisingly, there is no definition of the "perfect" team. There are teams, and the occasional combination of team members that come together to deliver something close to perfection. There will be faults and weak points in every team. From Boards to football teams, despite a huge investment of time and effort in identifying the right talent for exactly the right position, there will be faults. Whether that fault is brought about by an individual, or an outcome of the combination of individuals, there is no perfect team (except maybe the Arsenal FC side of 2003/04). There will be those that contribute, those that do not, those that drive the team forward, and those that act as a handbrake on any potential progress.

Involvement in teams will require a much broader lens on your capabilities and how you can contribute than if you were operating as an individual. Your core skills may not be the skills required, and your normal approach to work may not be what is needed at that time and in that circumstance. Simply having awareness of this is the first step to being a positive contributor to any potentially successful outcome.

Like any group assignment, your success will be directly intertwined with your ability to work with and guide these personas and the innumerable others you will encounter in any team setting. Your mindset must change from one where your natural reflex is to see a group assignment as a major inconvenience, to thinking of it as a complex interplay of personalities that must be mastered in order to unlock success.

And in a worst-case scenario, being part of a team does afford you the benefit of pointing at someone else when others are looking for who to blame. It's what got me through my tertiary education anyway.

The art of self-preservation

IN MY TRAVELS through the working world, I have come across a range of variations in terms of the culture of business. It's often the case that businesses are defined by their slight differences rather than their vast similarities. Overwhelmingly organisations look, sound, feel and — on occasions — smell slightly different wherever you go. Every business, be it large or small, is defined by a range of functional, cultural and operational nuances and variations.

One major tech company may be subtly different to the next, although they seemingly offer the same product or service. The same could be said for restaurants, bars and insurers. You'll often stumble across people who have come from a near-competitor, and they're overwhelmed by how differently their new place of employment may operate. From processes and principles to culture and leadership, those seemingly insignificant differences are often stark, dislocating and revealing. It's disconcerting to anyone who is new to a business, particularly if that person has fallen into the trap of being somewhat institutionalised by their previous place of work. Things just feel wrong or uncomfortable at first. There will be elements of their experience that will be better, but almost without exception there will be elements that are worse.

Now I'm not going to try and diagnose why these differences may occur — that's best left to overpaid consultants — but it is an inevitability that there will be a period of adjustment for any employer who joins a new place of work. And you should expect to experience this too, no matter how technically skilled or professionally experienced you may be.

But there is one thing that is inevitably consistent in every working environment — the need for self-preservation.

So much of our life hinges on our work. Work is a key part of our identity, it enables our life outside of work, and it impacts overwhelmingly on your physical and mental wellbeing. And given the importance of those things on an individual's potential sense of distress or fulfilment, it's no wonder that people will generally veer towards self-preservation when push comes to shove in the working environment.

I've had the displeasure of being part of organisations large and small that have gone through temporary or near permanent stress and decline. Whether it's changing economic circumstances, industry modernisation, evolving consumer sentiment and demands, or simply bad management, organisations go through periods where teams and employees are impacted by the ebbs and flows of success or failure.

In those circumstances there is one inevitable truth that emerges — regardless of mission statements or organisational visions — and that is the rapid shift to self-preservation at all levels in a business. It is not universally true for all individuals, but it will inevitably be seen at every rung and within every division of an organisation. Sometimes it becomes apparent without the business being in distress. There is a whole tranche of people you will come across in the working world for whom self-preservation is the guiding light for all that they do.

The means in which it manifests can vary. For some it becomes — like I mentioned in my earlier chapter on "How to get ahead" — an inevitable rush to align themselves most closely with management and decision makers (the "ass-kisser" route). For others it will be in withdrawing into themselves in order to stay "off the radar". For others still, generally managers, it will manifest as an intentional effort to broadcast how irreplaceable they are.

But no matter how it comes to life, it will drive that individual's entire being. Every action and every reaction will be tied up in how they maintain their personal status quo and retain all of the benefits (most likely money and authority) that comes with their current position.

In fact, there is a high likelihood that you will fall victim to self-preservation tendencies at some stage. It may not be related to macro business decisions and influences, but it might just be because you want to avoid or take on a specific task or that you want to prioritise yourself over others to get that promotion or avoid that redundancy. The overwhelming urge to position yourself above your fellow human will drive your behaviour, all with the intent of benefiting oneself and preserving yourself from harm or from getting the chop.

It is human nature to try and position yourself in such a way as to secure your ongoing financial security when there is an increasing scarcity of it. And you should expect to see that in many of those around you. It is an outlier to experience a more noble peer step in when decisions must be made as to who stays and who goes, and the workplace will become a smart casual version of *The Hunger Games* when businesses start to decline, and roles are made redundant.

PART 4
Work culture is not what you think

The workplace is not a democracy

THERE'S THIS ASSUMPTION in most Western countries and cultures that your opinion counts for something.

Sadly, it's not true.

Business, largely, doesn't care what you think.

Many of us (but not a majority of us as it happens) have probably spent our lives in the sweet embrace of a democratically elected government, in a family unit that has (occasionally) considered our perspectives and needs in decision making and surrounded by people who are interested in or receptive to our perspective on any range of issues[17]. Or at least they've pretended to pay attention anyway.

The assumption that your voice may be considered in decision making at work is as laughable as the idea that humanity can only thrive under a democracy and will inevitably fail under an autocracy. Any inflated expectations you might have around how influential your opinion might be in decisions need to be put to rest here and now.

The concept of democratic decision making comes from the ancient Athenian interpretation of "direct democracy". This gives the impression that all voices are to be heard, and that all votes count in the final decision.

There are certainly some upsides to the concept of a democracy. I can't think of many of them right now but I'm pretty sure

---

17   Around 5.55 billion people live in some form of autocracy. That means around three in four people on the planet live in an environment where they either do not have a vote or their vote is impacted by the informal or formal exertion of power by their government to such a degree where that vote has minimal impact.
Bastian Herre and Max Roser (2013). "Democracy". Published online at ourworldindata.org/democracy

there have to be some given how long some countries have persisted with it as a preferred form of government. Those ancient Greeks seemed to know what they were doing, and they seemed to prosper for a period so that is evidence enough for me[18].

That's in stark contrast to how resolutions are made in a more contemporary working environment. Decisions are instead made in small groups, by inner circles, by individuals and through a flurry of messages between important people. They are not made by asking the masses. *Demos* (people) and *Kratos* (rule) are concepts that grow weary on the shelf in the Ancient History section of the library rather than making their appearance in any of the tens of thousands of books published on modern day business decision making or organisational design.

There will, of course, be the drip feeding of "your voice"-style team feedback loops, but that acts only to highlight the fact that your individual voice doesn't actually count for anything.

We've all been part of organisations where there are chronic employee shortages, fundamental management issues, basic safety concerns and blatant process inefficiencies. And correspondingly you've probably ummed and ahhed about whether you were going to be *that* honest about *that* thing in that survey or suggestion box. We also recognise the risk that your contribution might make its way into the inbox of someone important. It's inevitably a bad thing if those in authority find out that you were the one who wrote that somewhat critical comment in the employee feedback survey and you'll forever have your permanent employment record smeared by the fact you once said that your team was dangerously short of gloves or whatever it was you were bitching about.

But your voice — individually — means nothing. You and your teammates have probably raised these issues survey after survey, meeting after meeting, suggestion box slip after suggestion box

---

18 It's largely agreed that ancient Greece as an influential and prospering culture came to an end in around the second century BC. For the USA, that same decline didn't materialise until around 1,800 years later.

slip. It's only when the autocracy of business takes over that any real impact or change is felt.

Nothing will happen until someone actually in charge deems the issue important enough — either through fear of personal reputational risk by failing to do anything about it, or by recognising the opportunity for advancement through actually doing something about it.

You're far less likely to see a need to actually improve things for the people or organisation as a rationale for solving an issue. Fear of being pursued and prosecuted by the authorities remains a far more popular choice to spark action, but you should put to rest any misplaced idea you might have about the opinion of the masses actually influencing the actions and behaviours of a business.

At least in ancient Rome they made it super clear that slaves didn't have a vote. Businesses would never be that overt or blatant. They know that hope is an antidote to most employee unrest, so they'll hold the concept of your voice being important over your head like that metaphorical carrot hanging just in the donkey's eyeline.

You might also find it counterintuitive but the fact your opinion might not count actually provides a huge upside.

If you almost immediately dismiss the idea that you have any actual decision-making authority, it is pretty relieving. You can feel your shoulders drop a little, and the air circulating around your lungs a little more freely knowing that you're just a cog in the machine and that it's actually The Organisation that is most exposed.

Your influence won't come from being loud or through having the weight of decisions sitting on your shoulders — it'll come from understanding how decisions really get made. And if you're lucky, over time, you might even be invited into the room where actual resolutions are formed and agreed.

Sure, it might sting at first to realise our opinion on things doesn't matter. Most of us like to think we have some influence and that our ideas matter, that someone is listening. But once you accept the truth that business is rarely built to run on consensus it takes a weight off. You're not supposed to fix everything. You're not failing when your suggestions go nowhere. You're just playing your role in a system that was never designed to hear everyone equally in the first place.

That doesn't mean you stop thinking, caring, or pushing when it matters — it just means you can stop banging your head against a locked door. You become more strategic. You learn to choose your battles, preserve your energy, and recognise what's actually within your control. You figure out what's yours to own, and what belongs to those further up the chain of command. And you work out how best to work with them.

What you need to recognise is that a large part of your job is simply doing what others say — and that others are responsible for their decisions. The second part of that statement is the most critical. Sometimes you have to release yourself into the duty of others and be sure that those around you are aware of that — not in the manner of shirking responsibility, but more with the intent of ensuring that others are aware of the fact that you are simply carrying out orders.

It's critical to know where responsibility lies. One of the key responsibilities you will have is being able to determine when things are your fault or not. Every business has a chain of command. Sometimes that chain of command will ask you to do things that are wrong, incomprehensible or of questionable value. Your job is to understand that you are there to do it on behalf of the business, but that the ultimate responsibility doesn't sit with you. In fact, in many instances through your life in the working world you'll quickly come to understand that not even your boss agrees with the task at hand.

There are countless examples of situations where an order has come down from on high and layer upon layer of the business have had to gravely nod their head and just do what is asked of them. It conjures up an image of those horrendous scenes whereby the lieutenants and their staff are sending troops "over the top" to their inevitable death. There's a general somewhere that has determined that it's a good idea to send the minions into the machine gun fire, and the chain of command simply falls into line. In this analogy you're that wizened sergeant joining the naive conscripts rushing towards impending doom.

Just be sure to let everyone know you're doing it because someone up the chain told you so, and if it all goes wrong — hopefully not to the extent that you and your pals end up as fertiliser somewhere in the Belgian countryside — that all blame should sit with them. It's wishful thinking but understanding where responsibility sits is a critical part of being able to do your job, and surviving the slaughter.

As you progress through business, you'll find that "simply following orders" begins to evolve into "following orders after you help the decision-makers decide what those orders are." Now that is real growth and the sign of a maturing business — the ability of all people within the chain of command to influence the plan of attack. Maybe you'll be able to influence the orders that come from those inept leaders who don't know the true nature of the environment in which you're working. Maybe you'll even be able to put an end to that truly outrageous and dangerously out of touch demand that probably seems like a good idea when you're making decisions way behind the frontlines in the comfort of a boardroom somewhere. Maybe you'll scream and shout and protest the absurdity of it all and just end up as cannon fodder out there in a muddy shell hole somewhere, slowly bleeding to death alongside your buddies.

But at least you can say "I told you so"... assuming anyone is listening.

Case study: The Boaty McBoatface paradox

As I've discussed in the previous chapter, democracy sounds noble in theory — until you try it at work. If you've ever run a team poll to name a new project, you already know that democratic input often leads to the worst possible decision.

Whether it's something innocuous like asking the team to suggest names for the new newsletter, or something more dramatic like having the board vote on whether they should pursue that acquisition, the reality is that there is a direct correlation between the number of people involved in a decision and how bad that decision will be.

Look at democratically elected governments for instance. They're generally a complete shitshow and largely disliked by everyone. And yet, despite this track record, we keep trying to replicate democratic ideals inside businesses — often with disastrous results.

The lesson is that the more people you get involved in the decision the worse that decision. Giving the people a voice also has a nice little side effect of ensuring a whole bunch of people have their nose put out of joint because their preferred outcome wasn't the one that was selected.

Case in point: Boaty McBoatface.

If you want definitive proof of why asking the public (or your team) for input can go wildly off the rails, let me direct your attention to a beloved low point in British democracy: the 2016 Boaty McBoatface Incident.

There are innumerable detailed recountings of the incident across the internet, and I wouldn't do credit to the breadth of context, history and social groundswell that surrounded it in these few short lines. Needless to say, the UK public was asked to name a research vessel and with a vote nearly ten times that of the second placed option, the public voted for the vessel to be named Boaty McBoatface.

The powers that be, who had designs in typical British fashion on something far more grand and majestic for this research vehicle, had fallen victim to that most impudent and audacious of forces; the public. They were left scrambling to fix a branding disaster they had accidentally crowdsourced.

The lesson? The larger the group, the more unpredictable and chaotic the decision. See also: riots, social media comment sections, and elections. People en masse follow a path of being more and more unpredictable as the number of people involved increases.

So, before you launch a poll to name the new performance framework or ask your 50-person team what your Slack channels should be called, ask yourself: are you ready for Boaty McBoatface?

Consensus may sound inclusive, but it often leads to absurdity, mediocrity, or resentment. Sometimes the most effective way to make a decision at work is to simply make one — and to take accountability for it when things inevitably go wrong.

Understanding "Priority Number One"

THERE'S A COMMON TROPE wheeled out by the business community that organisations in some way consider, or even prioritise, humanity in its decision making. Perhaps you're even part of one of the many organisations that prescribes to the idea — on paper at least — that people are their greatest asset.

Well, that was a lie.

The first priority in any business is profit — everything and everyone will be tolerated until their presence threatens or in some way reduces the viability of Priority Number One.

Now there are slight exceptions to this rule in the form of publicly funded spending (aka government) and some not-for-profit organisations, but the vast majority of businesses exist to create returns for shareholders or owners, and anything that jeopardises that fundamental need will be quickly identified and removed without prejudice.

And business won't simply stop in removing anything that risks its never-ending search for greater profits. It will also look outward, and, like a virus, it will exhaust any and all avenues to increase its spread and profit-making potential.

Here's a very incomplete list of things that businesses have done to increase their profitability:

» Overturned child labour laws

» Discriminated against people based on gender identity, disability, race, age, pregnancy, religion and sexual orientation (as a start)

» Lobbied against environmental protections

- » Provided illegal payments to just about anybody in a position of authority including politicians and judges
- » Participated in wage theft
- » Illegally dismantled unions
- » Used indentured servitude to secure a workforce
- » Ignored public safety
- » Dumped waste into protected ecosystems
- » Destroyed first nations and indigenous artefacts and art
- » Intentionally lied to authorities about the damaging consequences of using their product
- » Killed people
- » Killed endangered animals
- » Killed ecosystems
- » Jeopardised the ongoing habitability of our planet

And on and on.

And it's likely you rub shoulders with the bad actors that are responsible for these misdeeds every day.

It is clear that as individuals we can't fix capitalism or the infinite search for ongoing and (ideally) exponential profits. Your role will be continually scrutinised on the basis that you are either contributing to the financial and commercial outcomes of a business, or you are eroding the potential of its financial and commercial objectives. You will also see things around you that may put pressure on your own moral compass.

Your task is to determine how far you will go, what corners you won't cut, what moral stance you won't ignore, and when to walk away. It's undeniable that a moment will come somewhere in your journey through the working world where you will need to decide how far you will go in becoming complicit in the actions of

The Organisation. You may not be able to stop the inevitable progress of the machine, but you don't have to voluntarily choose to become part of it.

Organisations and businesses do not have such scruples or moral quandaries.

There are almost no organisations in the world of any significant size and scale that have not pushed, prodded and sometimes completely crash tackled some of those moral and ethical values that you might have held dear. From child labour to environmental destruction, through to less obvious acts like changing shift logs and dismissing those under financial stress in a depressed jobs market, you will come face to face, shoulder to shoulder and hip to hip with businesses and individuals that make those decisions. There's no hiding from it. The best thing you can do is determine where your line is, what you are willing to give up, and what your contingency plan might be if an organisation takes it one step too far.

I have worked in organisations that have killed people, withheld wages, physically mistreated customers, and have implemented industrial scale initiatives to overcharge or underpay tens of thousands of people. No-one — to my knowledge — has ever been charged with criminal offences in those organisations for doing those things. Sure, some of those organisations have had to pay fines ranging from laughable to immaterial, sometimes corporate brands have been damaged, and — on very rare occasions — some people may have lost their job as a result of their actions.

But they have never been held to the same standards as you and I as individuals.

Neither should you expect that there will be justice or moral outrage to the degree that you may imagine might be deserved, if at all. And the sad reality is that my experience has largely been with organisations and businesses that are seen as acting in good faith, who "put customers and the community first" (or words to that effect), and who have continued to operate relatively untouched and unscathed. They see these faults as a reputational or commercial blip, and inevitably carry on with doing what they've done, maybe with a new policy here, and stronger governance there, and a training module (most likely) everywhere.

I've often pondered how I could have been a part of these scenarios whilst still being able to sleep at night. The answer is not a simple one. Inevitably there will be some element of cognitive dissonance for each of us in business at some stage in our career. I maintain that there will be employees from Enron who still insist they did nothing wrong, decision-makers at Arthur Anderson who feel they were in the right, and Board members at Purdue Pharma who still feel like they actually came up with a really good product, but it was just those who used it illegally who were the problem.

Work will ask us to do things that challenge our own moral and ethical value systems. The key is to understand when our own personal beliefs and professional actions are so contradictory that we must start to adjust our beliefs en masse to rationalise those actions, or whether we remain content with the fact that we maintain beliefs that are in conflict with the things we do during our working career. These are our only two options, because it remains highly unlikely that you will work for an organisation that mirrors exactly your own belief system.

Prepare for the propaganda

THOSE OF US who have grown up in the Western world have an assumption (albeit a misguided one in more modern times) that "The Truth" is readily accessible — whether that be through a free press, social media or any other means of gathering information. Regardless of your political persuasions, we like to assume that we can access a balanced view on any potential news of interest, whether that be deeply researched articles interrogating a particular misdeed or controversy, a thoughtful commentary that scrutinises the issues to get to the root of the truth, or a balancing of the perspectives and knowledge of a vast range of fair-minded community members on your preferred social media platform of choice.

The naivety and reality in that assumption aside, you should be aware that there is no such thing as a free press — or The Truth — in the working world.

There is no journalistic integrity, there is no search to expose the awful truth, and there is almost no means — other than through rumour and innuendo — to try and access a balanced view of information that flows around a business.

Your manager, your manager's manager, your manager's manager's manager (etc.) is in no way incentivised to ensure that you and your colleagues have access to The Truth when it comes to the business. In fact, they probably have a significant interest in hiding The Truth from you. The last thing that The Organisation wants is for those who are most impacted by information (more often than not in a negative way) actually knowing what is going on.

In fact, you will come across a new language that I like to call LinkedInglish. The whole purpose of this language is to misdirect, deceive, misrepresent and deny the realities of what is happening in the business.

For instance, redundancies are often referenced as "structural resetting", "workforce rationalisation" or "efficiency finding".

I have even fallen victim to what was coined a "simplification".

Of the many workforce or cost reduction processes I have been part of in my career, there is not a single example where communication has been handled with transparency or honesty. Actually, if your business is big enough, it's likely that investors and the market will hear bad news before you do. It's simply the way things go.

Anything written or spoken under the guise of a Team Update or via an All Staff Town Hall is done with an agenda in place that is less about revealing reality and more about keeping the masses placated. If you actually want to find out why the front office lost thirty per cent of their staff in the last three months or why that news article spoke about a potential takeover from an Indonesian conglomerate, believe the "official" version at your own peril. What you're actually getting is a finely crafted (or maybe not so finely crafted) piece of propaganda designed to ensure you know just enough to limit any potential reduction in your productivity.

Politicians are rightfully chastised for bending, manipulating, forgetting or outright denying the truth, but at least some of us get to vote them out every few years (in theory).

As for what you'll see? You'll be getting the "Kim Jong-Il Treatment" from most organisations — unadulterated and uninhibited lies[19].

---

19 Kim Jong-Il, the now-deceased leader of North Korea, had a list of titles and roles that would make even the most creative LinkedIn influencer blush. Among them: Eternal General Secretary of the Workers' Party of Korea, Eternal Chairman of the National Defense Commission, and Generalissimo of the Democratic People's Republic of Korea. Not bad for someone who's been dead since 2011. Additionally, he was fantastic at crafting messages designed for the consumption of the masses — though "truthful" might be a stretch. For instance, he once finished an 18-hole round of golf at 38 under par, including at least five holes-in-one. Apparently, Kim Jong-Il got his start in communications.

There's also a very high possibility that as you progress through the corporate jungle that you will also be seconded into this half-truth telling and misdirection. In essence, there will be moments when you too will become complicit in the organisation lie-fest that surrounds business reshaping and downsizing.

You see, as you become more senior and are given more responsibility, your role will change from being at the receiving end of the communication, to being a broadcaster of the communication, and ultimately — should your career progress to the heady heights of decision making — to the manufacturing of the misdirection. You will be held accountable for its design, development and distribution. And just remember that if you're going to apply your ethics and decline the invitation to be part of the conspiracy, you too might find that you are facing the occupational firing squad, or, in LinkedInglish: looking for new opportunities as a result of a business wide organisational condensing and optimisation strategy.

Often, we are not given a choice as to whether we will become accomplices in the art of workplace misinformation. But you do have a choice as to whether the masses deserve to know something closer to The Truth. And for those of you who are not yet at the lofty heights of being tasked with the manufacturing of propaganda, you do always retain the ability to determine what you choose to believe, what you question, and what role you might have in helping interpret what The Truth may actually be.

The myth of business efficiency

THERE'S THIS COMMON assumption — most often peddled by those pro free markets and extreme capitalism — that businesses, in their never ending pursuit of financial returns, will continue to optimise their model to achieve greater and greater efficiencies.

When people stare up at these corporate monoliths and shrines to shareholder returns there's a natural assumption that this wealth has been built through the incredibly efficient utilisation of capital — be it natural, human or financial. The average Ali or Aisha would wander the streets of Shanghai and New York and London under the assumption that these massive organisations succeed and fail on the back of smart decision making, intelligent prioritisation and a forensic hunt for more and more ways to fine tune every element of the business.

As it happens, that assumption is complete bullshit.

Instead, organisations are often filled with contradictions, inefficiencies, and a near insatiable appetite to find ways to make things harder than they should be.

I have been in a variety of different KoolAid drinking sessions where this classic trope of businesses being surgical in their operation and management have been wheeled out. I've sat in postgraduate lectures from professors who specialise in organisational design, I've been in boardrooms to hear from consultants about maximising operational efficiency, and I've heard from motivational speakers who've implemented globally recognised optimisation in superbike technical teams and deep-sea fishing operators.

But every business — and I mean *every* business — has some level of easily diagnosable and observable inefficiency. Every business has dead wood, whether it's people or processes or products. Every business has some level of absurdity around how they do things, manage things, measure things or plan things. It's an inevitability that within the structures of a business there is always some level of inefficiency and tomfoolery.

Every. Single. One.

And often, those that claim to feature the most efficiency and effectiveness are in fact the exact opposite. Massive organisations are some of the most inefficient of all. In fact, I'd posit that the larger and more global the business, the more inefficient. They might be good at insulating their clients and shareholders from seeing it but have no doubt inefficiencies will be there somewhere — either out in the open for all to see or hidden in some corner like a malignant tumour growing unchecked. Whole teams, investments and individuals are insulated from the prying eyes of those out there in the wide, wild world. They have a vested interest in presenting themselves as highly adaptable, concise and efficient users of resources.

Inefficiency is often baked into the DNA of large organisations.

We've all wondered out loud how fundamental processes like ordering stationery or hiring people can become arduous, tedious and time consuming. And that's just the tip of the iceberg. Most people assume that organisations that fail do so because inefficiency has somehow crept into an otherwise highly efficient operating model. The truth is that they fail because inefficiency has finally overwhelmed and swamped anything that resembles operational effectiveness.

If big businesses were so efficient about teaching efficiency, how come consultancies still exist? How come they haven't published the "Secrets to Efficiency" handbook and essentially ended all wasted time, money and resources across business? You know the answer. They can't end it because it's not possible and it's not good business. They feast on it and exist because of it. And as for consultancies, well they're normally a hotbed of cronyism, myopic thinking, overwork and institutionalisation so they're by no means a point of reference for what good practice looks like.

In fact, most businesses are just a series of incredibly inefficient processes all somehow being held together by some IP or vertical capability or monopolistic positioning that pacifies the absurd ineffectiveness of the remainder of that organisation.

If there was a global award for "The World's Most Effective and Efficient Business", trust me when I say that none of the businesses you recognise by name would win; assuming of course that it was truly objective and based on recognising the meanest, leanest, smartest processes and methodologies.

The actual winner would probably be some micro-business hidden in a side street somewhere in Lagos or Istanbul or Delhi. A handful of super-efficient team mates each specialising in their area of expertise, each process they execute driven by efficiency of time and effort, and the outcome a perfect product or service that is delivering just the right level of practical benefit and customer love for each and every person that walks through the doors. It's also probably zero waste and a key cog in a circular economy. A perfect utopia of equality, efficiency and mutual benefit (and hopefully equal pay).

It's highly unlikely to be a business that has an immediately recognisable brand, or a bunch of shareholders, or clients dotted all over the world, or even "middle managers".

But even down to the smallest business (those hypothetical exceptions in Lagos, Istanbul and Delhi aside) there is some level of inefficiency; like why the hell does Susan drive all the way into the office AND THEN head out to get coffee FFS?!?

No business is perfect; what you choose to do when you see that imperfection is up to you.

And never assume that it's intentional.

Case study: Inefficiency in practice

As I've touched on in the previous chapter, inefficiency exists in almost every single business. And when I say "almost every single business" I don't mean like 85 per cent or 99 per cent, I mean like every single business except maybe two in the whole world.

I've seen, and been part of, my fair share of inefficiencies but one particular example really stuck out for me. It's a real-life case study in just how deeply inefficiency can embed itself in an organisation, and how a seemingly single point of inefficiency has tendrils that can have far wider impacts that we could ordinarily assume.

Many years ago, I was working for a fairly vast, national organisation. Due to some factors I can't quite recall, this particular business was going through a period of "budgetary constraint" (also known as "not spending money"). Budgets were being reviewed, reduced and scrutinised in every nook and cranny of the organisation. No new headcount, executives now flying economy (yeah it was that bad), vendors being squeezed and scope being reduced.

The level of scrutiny had found its way down to something as granular as printing costs. This business — prior to this new period of austerity — had relied on the support of an external printing company to produce documentation en masse. I can't recall the specifics of the documentation, but I recall there was a huge amount of pages per document, and there was an insane number of these documents adding up to thousands upon thousands of pages.

The previous method had been to load the document file on a USB, walk it down to the local printing company, pay the invoice (several thousands of dollars), and pick up the documents bound, sorted and boxed up some 72 hours later. It was essentially a one-person job, especially if they had a trolley or something wheeled to move the tomes back and forward from said printer.

But now that process had to change. The budget for printing was gone, but alas, the documents were still required — so an effective solution had to be found. Cue: absurdity and counter-intuition.

The final solution that the brains trust came up with looked a little something like this.

The documents would be produced in-house, given that the use of internal printers, ink and paper was carried as a building cost and hence would not require a discretionary budget.

A small army of team members was mobilised, given that this job was deemed so fundamental to the ongoing viability of the business that having them jump out of their day-to-day tasks was deemed appropriate. A group of those team members would be responsible for pushing documents out from their desktops to the printers scattered throughout the building. Another posse of team members would be responsible for manually collating and binding the documents; the third group would proof check that the second group had done their job correctly; and the final group would be responsible for packing the documents in archive boxes that had been commandeered for the job at hand.

And viola — job done and no pesky budget required. Suck on that Finance Team!

Of course, it did mean that every printer was unavailable across the three floors for about a week, that around 15 team members were "otherwise engaged" for a total of around 600 working hours, and that office costs for things such as paper and ink had rapidly spiked for a few days well beyond the costs of getting a third-party printing company to produce it. But job well done. It had been delivered "for free", and the team leaders were heartily congratulated for getting it done without the need for budget.

As a result of this extraordinary cost saving, the next time around we mobilised a team of contractors — at a premium — to do it all again, all in the spirit of cutting costs. For everyone else, they'd simply have to plan their printing needs accordingly.

The meritocracy myth

MERITOCRACY (NOUN):

"A social system, society, or organisation in which people get success or power because of their abilities, not because of their money or social position."[20]

A world based on ability and merit.

Oh my God, can you imagine?

It's hard to comprehend a reality where management made decisions about who gets fired or promoted based on their actual ability. Instead, let's travel all the way back to a place we call Earth.

The idea of a meritocracy seems to make perfect sense on face value. Surely any sophisticated social system, community or organisation should be capable of — and willing to — reward individuals based on their abilities? That sounds perfectly reasonable to me.

I hate to be the bearer of bad news, but now is the time to completely dismiss the concept that there is some kind of equilibrium between good people and good outcomes, and bad people and bad outcomes, *especially* in the working environment. The concept of a meritocracy does not exist.

I'm afraid there is no cosmic, karmic balance sheet here or anywhere.

I assume that the very origins of the concept of people being measured and rewarded on their merit has some kind of religious undertones. The idea that those who are evil are rightfully smit-

---

20   Cambridge Dictionary. "Meritocracy". Published online at dictionary.cambridge.org/dictionary/english/meritocracy

ed, and those who are good ascend to utopia (with a period of being burned really badly in purgatory in some instances) seems completely rational. We inherently believe that good begets good, and bad begets bad, and that this relatively simple equation can be applied to relationships, work, the next round of drinks or, indeed, our everlasting afterlife.

There's a more recent precedent that defines our expectation around being measured based on our ability. Many of us travel through our formative years in a structured school environment where we often know how we're placed based on measurable, objective criteria. You boast to your friend that you've done better than them, and cry to your parents that you'll study harder in the future. You know you're good at maths or bad at English. You and those around you have a clear picture of where you stand on the educational ladder. You know you're up the top, somewhere in the middle, or down the bottom somewhere.

Then you might choose to move into further education and once again you've got a numerical method by which to understand how you compare to your peers.

Finally, you enter the working environment, and everything that felt so familiar to you suddenly disappears.

You don't know *how* you're being measured, you don't have a clear picture on *what* you're being measured on, and on many occasions you don't even know *who* you're being measured by or against. You're really operating in a vacuum when it comes to how you're performing. Most workplaces don't have any form of meaningful, empirical measurement (maybe some sales roles aside) — and they'll deliberately avoid doing anything as overt as giving you a score out of a hundred or a rating on the A through F scale.

So not only do you have very little means by which you can be measured, suddenly everything becomes based on subjective opinion, limited observations, social networks, prejudices, and just a general "vibe".

Sure, there are performance reviews and customer feedback surveys if you're lucky, but ultimately the criteria by which you're judged is anything but based on merit or ability.

And that suits The Organisation perfectly.

I know that we all want to believe that the workplace is fair. If you were to believe the management books and professional networking sites you could easily fall into the trap of assuming that the hustlers and grinders, the conscientious studiers, the smart contributors and the savvy networkers were all on an inevitable path to success.

Correspondingly you've fooled yourself into thinking that the connivers and liars, the lazy and the impatient, the mean and the disturbed are going to be found out, weeded out and forgotten.

Well, it's sadly just not true.

Capitalism, by its very nature, does not reward good will or positive vibes or being nice or whatever else you want to call it.

Instead, you must realise that you are playing a game that requires you to game the system to survive. You must build those networks, impress those managers, and (be seen to) deliver those major outcomes. And make sure you let everyone know when that happens.

Without doing these things you risk being seen as replaceable or dispensable.

Now the reasonable question would be: How does the idea of a business contradict the concept of a merit-based system?

I've mentioned before that the entirety of your existence in the working world — at its most basic level — is categorised as "wages" on a spreadsheet somewhere. And as a result, organisations want to retain the maximum flexibility possible to make changes to that particular line. The foundations of any business relies on the minimisation of costs and the maximisation of profits, and as a result many decisions are made with that fundamental formula in mind.

Financials don't care about you. There's no *specific* need for you, your colleagues or your managers. Even the CEO is a temporary cost until a better alternative can be found to drive returns for owners (whatever form "owners" may take). Everyone will be tolerated until such time as a better profit-driving or cost-reducing alternative can be found.

Having been on the receiving end of organisations making decisions based on the financial circumstances of the day, it can be a rude realisation that any perceived goodwill on behalf of either party will be superseded by financial needs. When push comes to shove, your relationship with managers and leaders may be the only thing that ensures your survival when The Organisation demands that costs be reduced. It's the reality of how business decisions are made.

Critically, others around you understand this and use it to their advantage. And they also know that the definition of their value is not limited to the idea of being the best at their job. Decisions about who stays and who goes — despite the fundamentals of the financial equation — are made by people.

Therefore the task becomes positioning yourself effectively with those who are making decisions around you. Don't do it for them, do it for you. It might secure you promotions and better pay. It may also mean you keep that job when the business is rapidly falling back to its most basic need in reducing costs and maximising profits.

Having said that, it's not all doom and gloom, so let's look at the counterargument that might give you some hope when it comes to your experience in any given business. The reality is that organisations do place some importance on concepts like engagement, collaboration, diversity, camaraderie and cultural alignment. It's true that those things are only important because they increase productivity, retention and recruitment, but they do exist in most organisations. From family-owned shops through to global corporations, businesses recognise the value of having good people who create good results, which in turn create good financial outcomes. Hopefully that helps you sleep better at night.

So ignore any fairy tales about the best people staying and the worst people going. Because that's not the way business works, and the sooner you come to grips with that, the easier it will be to understand your place in the working world.

Other helpful terms that might explain what you're seeing

IN THE PREVIOUS CHAPTER we were able to review and dismiss the concept of a meritocracy as the prevailing force in how organisations recognise individuals and their relative importance to its success. Let's now explore some other terms that might better explain how organisations and the people in them might fail or succeed in the workplace. Feel free to determine which concepts best describe your place of work or current working relationships.

My intention here is to help put a label to some of the decision-making processes and influences that are swirling around in your place of work, in the hope that by identifying them and labelling them you will better understand what is taking place and how you might be able to react to their presence.

My hope is that with greater knowledge you'll be able to better label, interpret and react to the things that are happening to you and your colleagues. I've certainly benefited from being able to identify the forces at work around me, because once you see them you can't unsee them. Feel free to use this glossary in order to broaden your own knowledge or refer back to it if you're trying to diagnose your own situation.

Autocracy

Definition: A form of government where power is concentrated in the hands of one individual.

In life and work: We've covered this concept in some detail, but in summary it explains why those in a position of power have no obligation to consult you or anyone else about their decisions. You will learn this lesson quickly and come to understand that your circle of influence is probably much smaller than you assumed.

Business does not prescribe to any form of democratic decision making, so get used to being told rather than asked.

Plutocracy

Definition: A society that is ruled or controlled by people of great wealth or income.

In life and work: Wealthy people live by different rules to you and me. They do not see you as being the same as them, and they wield far more direct control than you can ever imagine. From policing to policy making, money makes the world go round. This is no different in a work environment where those on the big bucks get to make the big decisions, and those on the small bucks, well, we just play along.

Nepotism

Definition: Those with power or influence favour relatives or friends.

In life and work: You will be judged on factors outside of your specific expertise or ability to do the job, and one of the most critical factors in your success is being a relative or buddy of those who make decisions. You'll see people promoted because of their surname or partner, and you should never assume that talent alone determines success. They are dealt a different set of hands in this game we call life, and you probably didn't get dealt in at all.

Confirmation bias

Definition: A tendency to interpret new evidence as confirmation of existing beliefs.

In life and work: People will hear, see and read stuff that will — in their mind — confirm their own beliefs. That means anything you say is unlikely to impact on their strongly held views, and many people you deal with are simply never going to agree with your perspective, no matter how sensible that view may seem. More often than not they will see most evidence as verification of their perspective, and anything or anyone that doesn't agree with them will be labelled faulty, dubious or wrong.

Halo effect

Definition: The tendency for a perception in one area to influence opinion about another area.

In life and work: Just because someone is good at one thing doesn't make them good at another thing, and vice versa, and so often entire reputations are based on one or a very small number of actions — be they good or bad. That reputation can follow you or others for years. And businesses tend to view themselves as good at everything, despite extensive evidence to the contrary.

When it comes to interpersonal relationships you may see people who are technical experts become managers, and people who are good managers attempting to act as technical experts. As for the solution to that problem? Patience and resilience.

Self-serving bias

Definition: The belief that individuals or organisations are successful because of their own abilities, and that faults or failures are a result of external factors.

In life and work: People are very keen to claim all the glory for any successes, and far less keen to claim accountability when things go completely wrong. It's not because of their ineptitude or lack of leadership, it's much more likely due to ineffective project management support or a distinct lack of the right talent in the people around them to get the job done. Well, that's if you ask them anyway.

Affinity bias

Definition: The tendency for people to favour those who look and sound like them, whether that's due to similar interests, age, backgrounds or experiences.

In life and work: The ability to progress in business is directly impacted by how much you "fit in" with those around you, and to those people who are empowered to make decisions about your future. People unconsciously feel more comfortable with those people that somehow mimic elements of their own psychology and physiology, and those that don't have additional hurdles to overcome to survive and prosper in business.

This talks more broadly to "cultural fit" that is espoused with the same enthusiasm as "cultural acceptance". These two concepts may be at odds with each other but that doesn't prevent organisations from trying to do both things at once with varying levels of success.

Attribution bias

Definition: The likelihood that people make errors when they try to find reasons for other people's behaviour.

In life and work: People around you will always be looking for reasons as to why things happen, and they tend to default to assumptions that are inaccurate. No matter how you behave and act, people will draw assumptions about why you are behaving or acting in a particular way that are incorrect or misrepresentative. Sometimes you're just focused on your work, but they'll assume you're angry or hungover or whatever. Mind you sometimes they might be right...

Conformity bias

Definition: The act of matching attitudes, beliefs and behaviours to group norms.

In life and work: Whether it's in the playground or the lunch room, people have a bias towards being part of the majority. Individuals and businesses are often apprehensive or resistant to perspectives and opinions that are different to the accepted norms, and differing views will be treated as an outlier and those of a disruptor.

This can limit the willingness of people in business to absorb and consider perspectives that are in contrast with the prevailing perspectives of the masses. Conformity is often rewarded, whether or not it is the right thing to do.

Status quo bias

Definition: A preference for an individual or group of individuals to maintain their current state of affairs in preference to making changes.

In life and work: Similar to conformity bias, businesses and people feel much more comfortable doing the things that feel consistent with what they are currently doing and have always done. Change is hard both emotionally and practically, and the majority of people will react negatively to any change to how things happen today.

Continuing with the status quo is an almost imperceptible but all too common risk within organisations. The idea that we should continue to do things how they have always been done severely limits innovation, initiative and continual improvement. See the chapter entitled "Acting like an ADILT" for a deeper analysis of this particular bias.

Authority bias

Definition: The tendency to attribute greater accuracy to the opinion of an authority figure.

In life and work: The idea that authority figures have a much more sophisticated ability to make good decisions is questionable at best. Corporate and human history is littered with stories of how entire groups of people blindly followed the decisions of those in power, regardless of the quality of that decision making. Business is a hot bed of this thinking so expect to come across a combination of sycophants and the mindlessly compliant in any organisation, submitting to the will of those more senior than them. As to whether you join them, well, that's ultimately up to how much you like staying employed.

If it seems easy, it's because you don't know enough about it

IF SOMETHING LOOKS easy, it's probably because someone spent years getting good at it — not because the task itself is easy.

But that doesn't stop us from thinking we could carry out that task with the same level of expertise regardless of our own abilities and experience.

We've all sat in front of our screens and marvelled at the majesty of the Olympics or Wimbledon. We've all watched a chef craft and dollop and smear his or her way to something mouthwatering that verges on the brink of being witchcraft. And we've all probably watched a golfer golf, or a drummer drum, or a restauranteur restaurant and thought to ourselves "that doesn't look too hard".

Well, bad news. You — like me — are probably a naive fool.

We're hardwired to confuse what looks effortless with what must be easy. But here's the thing about that mindset — it's not just a harmless little moment of wishful thinking. It's a trap we carry with us, especially into our working lives.

Inverse correlation between (perceived) ability to do the job and understanding of the job itself is a really interesting affliction of the human condition.

To put it simply, if it looks easy, you're probably going to be bad at it.

And yet we keep falling for it. It's been happening forever. Too often we watch someone else do a thing and think, *yeah, I could probably do that too.*

Rarely do we leap to the conclusion that the reason it looks easy is because that person has spent so much time crafting their skills, refining their talents, and experiencing failures and successes in order to master their craft. We tend not to think, *wow that person must have put hours and hours of work into honing their skills in order for it to look so natural and accessible and understandable to me.*

The reality is that what looks easy most likely looks easy because someone knows far more about it than you do.

Be it preparing a legal brief to keep a client out of jail, replacing that keg to keep the frat boys from rioting, or flicking those switches and knobs in just the right way to get that plane flying, the reality is that it's so fucking unlikely that you could just step in and do it to the same level as that person you are observing as to make it almost impossible — despite what Hollywood might have you think (on the landing-a-plane thing anyway).

This assumption becomes especially dangerous when you're starting out in your career or stepping into a new role. Because the more you think something's easy, the less likely you are to actually learn how to do it well.

When you enter the working world there is a huge danger that your hubris, ego or naivety will inadvertently lead you to assume you're as capable as everyone around you — no matter what your experience. The truth is that there is a huge benefit in accepting the fact that you may not be as knowledgeable about the specific task at hand. In fact, it's a good idea to assume that you're useless to begin with.

So much has been written about social media as to make anything I might add to the conversation immediately forgettable, but when you look at it in the context of the working world it does throw up some interesting implications. With short form videos, long form content, a plethora of comments in varying degrees of helpfulness, and everything in between just an app or click away, humanity is now exposed to so many examples of other people creating and solving and producing just about anything you can think of. There are hacks and shortcuts in five second bites thrust into your feed, and as a result, everything that seemed so difficult or unknown to generations in the past is now there in 4K for you to watch at your own speed. Want to see how that advert was made? Click here. Intrigued by how the judicial system works? Here's a thumbnail. Interested in the most successful quick service restaurant in the world and how they make it all so timely and seamless? Here's a short video with helpful infographics and cartoon characters all tied together with an upbeat AI voice over.

And while that access is amazing, it has a weird side effect. The end result is that everyone thinks they're an expert. And it's rapidly bleeding into the working world. I think I've seen enough videos and GIFs to expertly perform open heart surgery. And making the perfect scrambled eggs? C'mon, give me a real challenge.

Social media has provided a platform for the normalisation — and indeed the demand — for narcissistic behaviour. And this narcissism normalisation has spread its roots into your physical and digital professional network.

We've got armies of people who think they know better.

If you want to test this hypothesis just work in retail or hospitality for a few weeks. It's odd they even bother with training in those industries given there are so many customers willing and able to tell you how they could do your job better than you do.

So remember, if it looks easy, start by being smart and acting dumb. Open your mind up to the fact that things may not be as easy as they seem or appear at first glance. Allow yourself to listen and learn. Give yourself time to master things. Perfection is rarely, if ever, the outcome the first, the second or the hundredth time around. Hell, you might even be willing to be wrong a few times so you can avoid inadvertently making yourself look like an idiot because you thought you knew it all.

And on the subject of perfection, it's always been perplexing to me that the working world as a whole is so fickle when it comes to doing things perfectly.

At school or university no-one sees it as a failure if you get a B+ or a credit (some extreme parents aside). In fact, I would celebrate just passing some subjects as a wild success. But strangely, when you get into the world of business there is very little acceptance of anything but perfection. We don't celebrate the 80 per cent of the project that we were able to deliver, and we don't focus on the three thousand drinks we did get to the table before we dropped a tray of martinis, but instead we gravitate towards the things that weren't done successfully. It's weird and I hate it, but it's the reality. And you should get used to it too.

Having said that, the good news is that the requirement for perfection drops off dramatically the more senior you get. There are CEOs who are widely applauded when they get one acquisition across the line (regardless of actual benefit to the customer) whilst they've overseen the complete failure of ten other attempts. And don't get me started on the success rate of IT system implementations (it's about one in three by the way).

And while perfection gets plenty of airtime, especially at the bottom of the org chart, there's something far more dangerous that flies under the radar — overconfidence.

Don't be that person who assumes they've got it all figured out. Don't be the one who clumsily dives in, only to hurt yourself, your colleagues, the business or your chances of success.

And I say this with the best intentions. Not fucking up is, strangely enough, one of the best ways to succeed.

So when in doubt, act like the dumbest person in the room. Not because you are — but because you're smart enough to know you might not be that smart. Yet.

Like all good things this particular psychological ailment has a formal name — The Dunning-Kruger Effect.

Dunning-Kruger Effect (noun):

> *A cognitive bias in which people wrongly overestimate their knowledge or ability in a specific area. This tends to occur be-*

cause a lack of self-awareness prevents them from accurately assessing their own skills.[21]

You're likely already familiar with the work of Dunning-Kruger. Whether it's watching your handyman expertly apply that coat of paint to the window frame or a colleague navigating their way around the digital leave request form, you've probably assumed — at least once — that you could do it just as well.

This is an important bias that you should be aware of in your own life, but it's when it comes to life in the working world where things get really important and a little personal.

With the Dunning-Kruger Effect in full force in your business you're now faced with lawyers acting like copywriters for the next sales brochure and commercial teams looking down their nose at the HR professionals thinking they've got it so easy (they probably do by the way). Maybe, like me, you'll even be told by some executive that their niece is doing graphic design at the local college so they could probably manage that marketing campaign if required.

The Dunning Kruger Effect means that everyone thinks they're an expert — not just in their own field.

You won't stop it. But knowing it's there? That's a start. Because when you realise everyone's quietly underestimating everyone else, you can also learn to spot the people who actually know what they're doing.

---

21 *Psychology Today*. Published online at psychologytoday.com/us/basics/dunning-kruger-effect

Acting like an ADILT

IF YOU ACCEPT THAT you know nothing, then your mindset changes.

Suddenly you are on the hunt for understanding, rather than assuming you know. You want to observe and absorb how and why people do things around you, and that can only benefit you. It will invite you to ask questions and watch those who are more knowledgeable, and that will only benefit you as you become the one that has to complete the task.

But like everything, there is a flipside to this, and that's where the Always Done It Like That (ADILT) bias makes itself known.

Every organisation and employee has at some stage fallen victim to the ADILT mentality. Humans love predictability and patterns. We love the comfort that comes from being able to simply rinse and repeat tasks. It requires less brain power, it reduces perceived risk, and it brings comfort through constant repetition and predictability.

It also means that we're less likely to look for efficiencies or alternatives. It means that we default to what has come before, and it means we overestimate how effective it is to keep simply doing things the way we've always done them.

The danger isn't just starting out too confident. It's getting too comfortable too soon. Because once you've figured something out, your brain wants you to stop there. That's how the ADILT trap gets you.

So herein lies the balancing act.

The process might look something like this:

You start out decidedly incompetent watching someone do a task and assuming it can't be that hard.

You realise you actually want to understand it, so you begin learning how to do it properly.

You start doing the task and gradually improve until you're competent (not expert — just not embarrassing).

Then you hit a fork in the road:

a. The ADILT deviation: You get good enough to coast. You stop improving. You repeat the task over and over because that's how it's always been done. Eventually you get bored, start listening to audiobooks, and maybe begin taking notes for a future witty book using your ill-considered observations about workplace dysfunction, or;

b. The continual improvement deviation: You use your growing knowledge to rethink and improve the task. Whether it's perfecting the soft-serve cone or revolutionising a digital process. This is where the real value — and satisfaction — lives.

Your boss profits either way. But if you play it smart, you might just leverage your work into a pay rise — or at least into not getting fired next budget cycle.

I will say that the above process is far from perfect. At any point things can go wrong. You may be incompetent or uncoordinated. The process may already be perfect, and your suggestions are stupid and ineffective. Your boss may be a real pain-in-the-ass, and they may just keep all the benefits to themselves and leave you with nothing more than a really impressive process improvement and an empty bank account. I could also be full of shit and none of this will realistically make a difference of any sort and you're just in a dead-end job where nobody cares and nobody appreciates anyone doing anything differently from what has always been done before.

Still, if you want to improve your odds of being successful, being curious beats being cocky or comfortable every time.

Case study: The hole in the wall

I REMEMBER ONE of the jobs I had when I was at university was to work in a very luxurious five-star hotel that featured a name that you would most likely recognise and that many — myself included — would aspire to stay in. The General Manager rolled in one day like some sort of pseudo celebrity to chat to the cohort of slightly awkward looking new starters who were receiving their induction. We were all sitting in our misshapen, ill-fitting uniforms, still naive as to how things *actually* ran in that sort of organisation, waiting for the message from on high to inevitably draw us closer into the bosom of the "corporate culture".

And this guy starts by saying all the normal stuff; things like, "I'm super excited to welcome you...I started at the bottom and now I'm here...there's plenty of opportunity for you to grow", etc.

And then he said something that stuck with me. So let me share with you my hazy, 20-year aged memory of what he said.

"You know there are plenty of us who've worked here for a long time, and we've benefited to some degree from the familiarity that the everyday provides us.

"But sometimes we forget that we once walked past a huge hole in the wall and thought to ourselves 'gee, someone should fix that hole in the wall.'

"We then walked past it the next day and said to ourselves, 'Today I'm going to get that hole fixed'.

"Then we walked past it the next day, the next day, and so on and so on until we forgot there was a hole in that wall.

"Well, you guys are all starting your journey here today, and I'm asking you to look around as you go and to tell us where those holes in the wall are."

It was incredibly powerful to me as a young person just starting my journey in the professional world. Here was this hotel GM for a globally recognised brand asking me whether I could let him or one of his team know about these huge gaping holes in the wall. He was telling me that even he was blind to some of the really obvious issues in this massive — and presumably highly efficient — luxury hotel.

Fresh eyes (and what happens next)

So go out there and tell others about any holes in the wall. One of the first things I tell people who are starting in a new organisation — especially if they're starting in one of my teams — is that they have a huge privilege in being new. They're seeing things for the first time. They're recognising and interpreting how things are done. They're wandering the hallways for the first time looking for holes in the wall that we may have just grown used to, or we've convinced ourselves are a "feature", or that we've simply lost the will to fix.

Now here's the rub though. Not everyone wants to hear about the hole in the wall. Not everyone is mature or self-assured or objective enough to recognise that we've all got a role to play in identifying and fixing those things, and that those who are new to the business often have the best line of sight to identifying those critical inefficiencies or broken processes. Not everyone is like that hotel GM who saw it as an opportunity to improve the business rather than the potential to criticise the business and its people. Some people will take it personally, some will see it as a ringing indictment of everything they've stood for over the years, and some just won't give a shit.

I was going to put some kind of rhetorical questions here like "What kind of person are you?" or some cliche crap like "Strap on your overalls because today you're learning how to fix holes in the wall" but that's not what I'm here to do. If you want that kind of advice, go look up some LinkedIn influencers and their self-quoting and hashtags. I'm just saying sometimes there are holes in the wall that people have forgotten about, and what you do from there is up to you.

You'll see a hole. You'll decide whether to fix it, ignore it — or, like the rest of us, forget it was ever there.

PART 5
Where do we go from here?

The "perfect business"

IF YOU ASK Chief Financial Officers or business founders to outline their perfect business, it would look something like this:

Infinite revenues - zero costs = infinite profit

That's the reality. Any costs have an impact on profitability and should therefore be reduced to as close to a minimum as possible (aka $0).

So the reality is that you, as a contributing factor to that concept of costs, are actively limiting the ability for the financial team to zero out all cost lines, and therefore you have a negative impact on the overall profitability of the business from a purely commercial perspective. Beyond having to pay people there are also other pesky costs that creep in like facilities, health and safety, environmental, community and governance costs. These are all requirements forced upon a business by either a practical need to sell and produce a product or intellectual property, or to minimise the potential risk that the business presents to humanity and the ongoing viability of our planet.

If we lived in a land without laws around environmental protections, minimum wage, slavery, workplace safety or other legal obligations then that would be a perfect nirvana in the eyes of those who take a purely commercial view of the world. Anything else is — in their mind — a concession to the practical requirements applied (and forced upon them) by society.

As to whether they choose to follow the expectations of the judicial system, voluntary industry commissions and society as a whole is another question.

And this is the dynamic we find ourselves working in when we "voluntarily" sign up to work for any organisation. There is an inherent pressure to both reduce costs and maximise earning, whilst operating within the confines of the legal and ethical framework that all organisations must adhere to (mostly, anyway). And all of this happens under the auspices of generating as much profit as possible for The Organisation.

So how is it that we can position ourselves to be absolutely indispensable to an organisation when their needs are so stark and inhumane? The reality, of course, is that organisations of all shapes and sizes need people to operate them. There aren't any (yet) completely automated organisations that operate without any human intervention somewhere in their establishment or operations. Our task is to ensure that we are creating the most possible value for a business.

"Value" in this sense may come in a variety of different forms, but we must be able to draw a path from our efforts through to the creation of profitability.

Sometimes this path is non-linear. It may be that you are making processes more efficient (that contribute to more profit), it may be that you make the team more engaged and less likely to steal or abscond (therefore contributing to more profit), or you may be producing social posts that entice more people to shop with your business (therefore contributing to more profit).

Sometimes the role you play may be far more linear in the creation of value, such as working in sales. Sometimes you work in marketing and things are so vaporous that it's hard to draw any conclusion as to whether you contribute to profitability or not but that's another book entirely.

The short version is that profit creation is the language of love for organisations. We have to position ourselves so that it's understood that we are doing this, and clearly communicate the fact that we are contributing to the profitability of an organisation through the reduction of costs or the increase of revenues. That's the fundamental truth of any and all organisations. If this clear requirement is forgotten, misconstrued or ignored we rapidly become a target when others are making decisions about cost reductions or revenue increases (but mainly cost reductions).

People thrive in organisations for a range of reasons that I have outlined through this book. Sometimes it's because they are related to someone. Occasionally it's because they are lucky. But have no doubt that the most effective way to achieve success in any business is to clearly align your efforts with tangible outcomes that drive business profitability. Organisations will put up with a lot so long as they see this clear alignment between your efforts and their own, indisputable goals.

Remember, it is a transaction like any other; they want as much value for their investment as possible. Your wage is the investment, and the work that you do must clearly deliver on what they recognise as value.

PART 5: WHERE DO WE GO FROM HERE?

So what's important?

SUCCESS IN OUR WORK LIFE, and life more broadly, is a complex issue. For some people it is about contentment, for others it's about the accumulation of wealth. Let's look at the scale of what "wealth" might mean.

Have you got a million bucks?

Great, you're a million dollars away from having zero dollars.

And you're nine hundred and ninety-nine million dollars away from being a billionaire.

There are *at least* half a million homeless people in the USA, with estimates ranging up to 2 million when you include "sheltered homeless". At the other end of the spectrum there are less than 1000 billionaires in the entire continental USA.

Statistically, that means you're far more likely to be homeless than to become a billionaire — at a ratio of about 2000:1. In the world's most prosperous nation, you are 2000 times more likely to experience homelessness than to join the billionaire class[22].

Statistical likelihood tells us that you should have more of an affinity with those who are homeless than those who are billionaires. But somehow society spends far more time talking, thinking and dreaming about how to become a billionaire versus how we might be able to support those who are less fortunate.

But I digress. This book is about how you can survive and thrive in the workplace, not about social inequity.

So what can we learn about how we build our sense of self by using the billionaire to homeless ratio?

---

22   In fairness, there are also about 24.5 million millionaires living in the USA today. So it begs the question: how can so many have so much, yet homelessness continues to be such an inherent problem in the world's richest country?

Well, for one, you're more likely to be one than the other.

Statistically it would be wiser to interrogate what makes people fail (by capitalist standards) as compared to what makes them succeed. People fall into homelessness because of drug problems, family violence, mental health issues and sexual abuse (amongst other reasons). We should study those things more closely if we want to improve our chances of success. Why is it we're interested in what Elon or Jeffrey or Bill are doing when we still have a mental health pandemic and domestic violence issues sweeping our communities? Don't read *The Art of the Deal* until you've read online resources about how to support your mental health. Don't worry about *Rich Dad, Poor Dad* until you've been able to create psychological safety in your own home and life.

As for billionaires? Well, they're not billionaires because they are the hardest workers or put in the longest hours despite what the ghost writers of their autobiographies might want you to believe. They're not billionaires because they pulled themselves up by the bootstraps better and harder than you or their fellow man. The reality is they — almost without exception — had better connections, better timing, wealthier contributors and lower ethics than you. No one person can actually generate One Billion Dollars of value. That's just not possible. The best mechanic or cobbler or labourer will never reach a billion dollars through hard work alone. Clearly billionaires have relied on their ability to influence and manipulate those around them in order to unlock the capital created by those who sit under them on the pyramid. And most billionaires are fucking grubs who have no issue absorbing as much wealth as then can out of nature and humanity in order to feed their own egotistical needs. No-one actually needs billions of dollars — there is nothing on Maslow's Hierarchy of Needs that costs that much.

What does all this mean for you in the workplace?

For me, I have aspired for contentment rather than wealth. I have no jealousy when people tell me they're working so hard they don't have time for family, fun or friendship. I don't aspire to be a CEO if it requires me to sacrifice my own mental health or sense of psychological fulfilment.

So what is your goal? Wealth or contentment? And how does wealth look different when your ultimate goal is happiness rather than just having lots of stuff?

The workplace cares very little for your non-work aspirations (not even in those performatory emails from HR regarding Mental Health Awareness Week). But it does love the idea of workers mindlessly striving towards wealth, because more wealth is the only currency that work can offer. They need you to want a bigger house, a faster car and a more expensive holiday as long as you translate that into longer hours and more sacrifice in order to deliver more capital value (i.e. money) to them.

I've never aspired to have a certain amount of money in my bank account. I've aspired to live a happy, fulfilled life. I've experienced the burnout of aiming for wealth accumulation, and the dissatisfaction that comes with working for organisations and people that operate in complete contradiction to my own values. I made work my identity. It was only when I understood concepts about luck and the real priorities of any organisation that I realised that my dreams aren't a feature of any business plan or strategy document. That way work became a tool that I needed to manage as an input *into* my life, rather than it being the centrepiece *of* my life.

You'll be fine (probably)

DESPITE WHAT THIS BOOK might suggest, I have spent various moments of my working life enjoying what I do and appreciating the people I have shared the experience with. Much of what I have written is designed to be — such is the tone of much of today's dialogue — provocative and controversial. But I have always relied on some level of truth to form the foundation of what I have written. Whether that kernel of truth comes from my own experience, my observations, or conversations with others, everything in this book is grounded in truth — even if it's sometimes hard to spot beneath the layers of guff and pontification.

And some of those truths are unavoidable. Merit does not necessarily equate to opportunity, luck is a common trait of those who have achieved professional success, and the system really is fundamentally skewed towards The Organisation.

I'm also entirely aware that my own experiences and interpretations carry some level of misrepresentation and are unlikely to be common to all. I am not faultless and have never been in all aspects of my life, including my approach to work, but I have tried hard to present my own observations in a way that uncover some of the truth of my own experiences and the experiences of those around me.

There have been innumerable occasions during my own working life where I have needed the support of others to interpret and understand what I see, and I hope this book provides some kind of support in your time of need.

It's my hope that this book has provided some level of illumination to you about some of the circumstances you will find yourself in during your own journey through work. I also hope that it has offered you some tools and tactics through which to manage the weird and wonderful scenarios that work will manifest through-

PART 5: WHERE DO WE GO FROM HERE?

out your working life. If nothing else, you should congratulate yourself for making it through to the end of this book. We're generally terrible at celebrating success or completion in the professional environment, so take a moment to give yourself a pat on the back for ticking something off your to-do list.

My sentiment from my introduction to this book still holds true; that I hope you have been able to use this book in a way that suits your needs, not mine. Maybe you laughed (or at least smiled) on occasion, and perhaps something in here has helped you get through a tough conversation or a tough day.

Whatever it is, I've enjoyed sharing my thoughts and ruminations. Maybe it will give you the courage to do the same with those around you. There is too little frankness and honesty in the workplace, and finding your voice in a way that empowers you and those around you without getting any of you fired can be incredibly rewarding. Your observations, recommendations and interpretations have as much merit as mine, and we all benefit from understanding more about what we might face when we walk into the office or join that online call.

Finally, not all work is bad. You will make friends, you will feel joy, and you will experience great moments of optimism and achievement.

But you might have to jump off a cliff or two or navigate the Dunning-Kruger Effect to the point of exhaustion while you do it.

Wishing you all the best in whatever it is you do. And please try not to be an asshole.

Kind regards, and good luck!

RJF

2025

www.ingramcontent.com/pod-product-compliance
Lightning Source LLC
Chambersburg PA
CBHW072006290426
44109CB00018B/2153